Postsecondary Developmental Programs:
A Traditional Agenda with New Imperatives

by Louise M. Tomlinson

ASHE-ERIC Higher Education Report 3, 1989

Prepared by

Clearinghouse on Higher Education
The George Washington University

In cooperation with

Association for the Study
of Higher Education

Published by

School of Education and Human Development
The George Washington University

Jonathan D. Fife, Series Editor

Cite as

Tomlinson, Louise M. *Postsecondary Developmental Programs: A Traditional Agenda with New Imperatives.* Report No. 3. Washington, D.C.: School of Education and Human Development, The George Washington University, 1989.

Library of Congress Catalog Card Number 89-63439
ISSN 0884-0040
ISBN 0-9623882-2-X

Managing Editor: Christopher Rigaux
Manuscript Editor: Jean Shirhall
Cover design by Michael David Brown, Rockville, Maryland

The ERIC Clearinghouse on Higher Education invites individuals to submit proposals for writing monographs for the *ASHE-ERIC Higher Education Report* series. Proposals must include:
1. A detailed manuscript proposal of not more than five pages.
2. A chapter-by-chapter outline.
3. A 75-word summary to be used by several review committees for the initial screening and rating of each proposal.
4. A vita and a writing sample.

ERIC Clearinghouse on Higher Education
School of Education and Human Development
The George Washington University
One Dupont Circle, Suite 630
Washington, DC 20036-1183

This publication was prepared partially with funding from the Office of Educational Research and Improvement, U.S. Department of Education, under contract no. ED RI-88-062014. The opinions expressed in this report do not necessarily reflect the positions or policies of OERI or the Department.

EXECUTIVE SUMMARY

What Is Postsecondary Developmental Education?

Developmental programs at institutions of higher education encompass a variety of courses and services that are conducted to provide assistance to individuals who have been denied regular admission to the institution because of failure to meet specified admission and placement requirements or because of predicted risk in meeting the requirements of college-level courses. These services focus primarily on skills in reading, writing, mathematics, and study and test-taking strategies, as well as personal adjustment and other affective variables that are critical to success in the college curriculum.

How Have Developmental Programs Evolved?

In response to the needs of the underprepared student, programs classified as "college preparatory" since the mid-1800s have served many of the same goals as those programs that have more recently been labeled "academic development," "learning assistance," or "developmental studies." The change in the labeling of preparatory programs is, to some extent, associated with the change in student populations. Whereas socioeconomic status, instead of ability, was once the primary determinant of attendance at a college or university, the student population now admitted to institutions of higher education through developmental programs or the regular curriculum reflects a wide range of statuses in terms of race, ethnic origin, socioeconomic background, high school grade point average, age, and career objectives. A major factor in this diversity has been admissions policy in response to society's evolving perception of the role and value of higher education.

As a result of the growing diversity among enrollees at postsecondary institutions of learning, a number of developmental program models have emerged. Some of these models are comprehensive and some are specialized. There are at least four different types of program categories: college campus tutorial/remedial, college outreach programs, campus assistance centers, and off-campus instruction. The specific types of intervention involve the teaching/learning process, counseling, peer support, and supplemental use of media and the arts to develop students' articulation of basic skills and the application of those skills to various content areas in the college curriculum.

Of the numerous developmental programs across the nation, several can be identified as exemplars in terms of their success. Many programs, including those considered successful, have encountered a variety of problems, however. The continuous burdens that these programs face include problems of funding, staff recruitment and retention, admission and placement standards, minority student enrollment, the quality of tests, the relativity of curriculum, and perceptions of the program.

The evolution of academic assistance programs can be characterized as a progression from service for a small segment of the total population through the use of limited techniques and limited funds to service for a broad span of the nation's population by means of a more cohesive and comprehensive effort and the support of regularly budgeted programs. Expenditures for the administration of developmental programs vary across institutions and states and have ranged from $6 million for one state system to $12 million for one university. Approximately 90 percent of all institutions of higher education provide some developmental service, at least 30 percent of the national population in higher education is enrolled in some aspect of these services, and 33 percent of institutions report having a separate department or division for developmental studies or learning centers.

Postsecondary remedial education and its relationship to equity are often perceived to be in conflict with the desire to maintain high standards and cost efficiency. Although a substantial segment of popular opinion holds that developmental courses should be conducted exclusively at the two-year, community-college level, proponents of multilevel distribution of developmental services argue that even the best institutions in the nation have "low" students who benefit from such services. Senior colleges and universities house schools of education with faculty and graduate students specializing in the areas of remedial education and counseling, which are essential to developmental programs, and positive results have been reported in evaluations of services at two-year, four-year, and university levels. Moreover, two-year colleges have often experienced the same problems in their efforts to deliver remedial services as have other types of institutions.

Will Developmental Programs Decrease the Integrity of Academic Institutions?

Popular opinion often maintains that developmental programs dilute academic programs, but proponents of developmental programs argue that their role is to support and enrich the regular curriculum so that more students will succeed. Thus, remedial programs are perceived by their supporters as additions to, not replacements for, a required curriculum.

Postsecondary developmental programs have helped to fulfill the mission of providing equal educational opportunity in a democratic society. These programs have provided a "last chance" for many individuals to obtain worthwhile experiences in higher education that will enable them to find meaningful participation in employment and community life. Where institutions of higher education have had to strive to maintain a balance between the competition for student enrollments and a standard of excellence, developmental programs have helped to increase the pool of qualified incoming freshmen. Thus, the institution has served the community while serving itself.

What Is the Future for Postsecondary Developmental Programs?

Enrollment in developmental programs has increased in recent years, and the trend will most likely continue into the 1990s and beyond. Observable and projected changes in the diversity of levels of preparedness of high school graduates, sociological and technological change, employment trends, and other demographic factors will continue to create educational needs that will require higher education's commitment to developmental assistance.

New precollege curriculum requirements, new admissions and placement standards, and new trends in college curriculum will all create continuous need for academic support of college applicants who fall short of meeting the challenge of these changes. The preparation of teachers and administrators and the capacity of public policy to address these concerns will have to be monitored by long-term evaluation processes, which will add momentum to the refinement of developmental programs.

Emerging theories for training intelligence, enhancing intelligence, and using the application of philosophy to develop the art of thinking all hold great potential for meeting the challenges that lie ahead in developmental curriculum for verbal comprehension, visual/spatial problem solving, and the logic of communication—critical aspects of basic skills instruction and individual competence.

The impact of developmental programs will also be strengthened by administrative training for developmental personnel—currently recognized as a priority for developmental educators. The doctoral degree program in developmental education at Grambling University, for example, has recently incorporated a specialization in management in higher education, and institutions across the nation have negotiated to enroll their faculty in this program. Doctoral programs in developmental education are also in place at other institutions, and national organizations have been established to support professional endeavors for developmental personnel.

In regard to issues of program recognition, relativity of curriculum, and the prosperity of learning assistance programs, it may be advantageous for some programs to be incorporated into standing departments or schools on their campus. In this way, collaborative efforts in research and curriculum development may be more easily achieved and, in some cases, more substantial line-item funding can be obtained. Finally, if programs strive to identify sound internal and external evaluation procedures, and those procedures are used with objectivity, policymakers and practitioners will be better able to make informed and unbiased decisions about the improvement and direction of developmental programs for the future.

ADVISORY BOARD

Roger G. Baldwin
Assistant Professor of Education
College of William and Mary

Carol M. Boyer
Consultant and Senior Academic Planner
Massachusetts Board of Regents of Higher Education

Ellen Earle Chaffee
Associate Commissioner of Academic Affairs
North Dakota State Board of Higher Education

Martin Finkelstein
Associate Professor of Higher Education Administration
Seton Hall University

Carol Everly Floyd
Associate Vice Chancellor for Academic Affairs
Board of Regents of the Regency Universities System
State of Illinois

George D. Kuh
Professor of Higher Education
Indiana University

Yvonna S. Lincoln
Associate Professor of Higher Education
University of Kansas

Michael A. Olivas
Professor of Law
University of Houston

Richard F. Wilson
Associate Chancellor
University of Illinios

Ami Zusman
Principal Analyst, Academic Affairs
University of California

CONSULTING EDITORS

Robert Berdahl
Professor of Higher Education
University of Maryland

Kenneth A. Bruffee
Director, The Scholars Program
Brooklyn College of the City of New York

L. Leon Campbell
Provost and Vice President for Academic Affairs
University of Delaware

Charles S. Claxton
Associate Professor
Center for the Study of Higher Education
Memphis State University

Darrell Clowes
Associate Professor of Education
Viginia Tech

Susan Cohen
Associate, Project for Collaborative Learning
Lesley College

John W. Creswell
Professor and Lilly Project Director
University of Nebraska

Andre Deruyttere
Vice President
Catholic University at Leuven, Belgium

Mary E. Dilworh
Director, Research and Information Services
ERIC Clearinghouse on Teacher Education

Lawrence Erickson
Professor and Coordinator of Reading and Language Studies
Southern Illinois University

Irwin Feller
Director, Institute for Policy Research and Evaluation
Pennsylvania State University

Kenneth C. Green
Associate Director
Higher Education Research Institute
University of California at Los Angeles

Milton Greenberg
Provost
American University

Judith Dozier Hackman
Associate Dean
Yale University

Brian L. Hawkins
Vice President for Computing and Information Sciences
Brown University

Lynn G. Johnson
Executive Director
Hudson-Mohawk Association of Colleges and Universities

Carl J. Lange
Professor Emeritus
The George Washington University

Oscar T. Lenning
Vice President for Academic Affairs
Robert Wesleyan College

Judith B. McLaughlin
Research Associate on Education and Sociology
Harvard University

Andrew T. Masland
Judicial/Public Safety Market Manager
Digital Equipment Corporation

James R. Mingle
Executive Director
State Higher Education Executive Officers

Elizabeth M. Nuss
Executive Director
National Association of Student Personnel Administrators

Wayne Otto
Professor of Curriculum and Instuction
University of Wisconsin

Anne M. Pratt
Director for Foundation Relations
College of William and Mary

Karen T. Romer
Associate Dean for Academic Affairs
Brown University

John E. Roueche
Professor and Director, Community College Leadership Program
Sid W. Richardson Regents Chair
University of Texas

Mary Ellen Sheridan
Director of Sponsored Programs Administration
Ohio State University

Betty Taylor
Coordinator, Office of Educational Policy
New Jersey Department of Higher Education

J. Fredericks Volkwein
Director of Institutional Research
State University of New York at Albany

William R. Whipple
Director, Honors Program
University of Maine

Reginald Wilson
Senior Scholar
American Council on Education

CONTENTS

FOREWORD

There are two basic issues underlying discussions concerning academic development programs at the postsecondary level. The first is a debate over the legitimacy of higher education institutions having to offer these types of programs. Those who feel that academic development programs should not be part of postsecondary education take an idealistic, meritocratic position that is historically unsubstantiated. Their position can be thusly summarized: No student should apply who is not fully academically prepared for postsecondary education; it is the secondary and elementary schools' responsibility to adequately prepare students to go on to higher education.

While this position is admirable, it is not reality-bound. First, our national secondary school system did not come into existence until nearly 300 years after the founding of the first American college. As a consequence, American higher education has always had to help prepare some of its students to be academically capable for the intellectual rigor of higher education. Second, even with a national secondary school system, the quality of this system is so inconsistent that it is unrealistic to expect that all students who are intellectually capable of a postsecondary education will have received adequate training.

The second debate is to what extent should an institution of higher education provide academic development opportunities. In the 1950s and into the 1960s, the "revolving door" philosophy whereby students were admitted and then routinely flunked out if they couldn't meet the academic standards, is no longer acceptable in the 1980s and will not be acceptable in the 1990s. The national need for a well-educated labor pool will be so great in the 1990s that if our nation is to remain economically viable and competitive, every effort will be needed to insure that there is no waste of the intellectual resources of our youth. The point is not *whether* an institution should place resources in academic development activities, but *what* academic development activites are necessary in order to assist students to meet the necessarily rigorous graduation standards of our institutions.

In this report, Louise Tomlinson, assistant professor of reading at the University of Georgia, delineates the new conditions that make development studies such a compelling issue: changing student populations, renewed emphasis on civic responsibility, identifiable learning deficiencies, and falling standardized test scores. After providing an overview of the history of developmental programs, she goes on to identify characteristics of programs, examples of successful programs, and methods of evaluating programs.

As demonstrated by the author, when institutions carefully integrate academic development programs within their curriculum, the unnecessary tensions between those who have received adequate academic preparation and those who have not cease to be an issue. If this country is to maintain a strong educated citizenry, support for developmental programs both within and external from the institution must be nurtured. This monograph helps to develop such a foundation.

Jonathan D. Fife
Professor and Director
ERIC Clearinghouse on Higher Education
School of Education and Human Development
The George Washington University

ACKNOWLEDGMENTS

This work was initiated in part to fulfill a Sarah H. Moss Fellowship given to me by the University of Georgia to do research at Yale University.

I wish to thank Wayne Otto for inspiring me to write into the future, Leroy Ervin for providing faculty development workshops which encouraged me to examine some of the most recent philosophies in intelligence training programs, and Edmund Gordon for providing guidance and direction on the many facets of this report.

I would also like to thank Doris M. Backus, Esperanza Valdes, and the Goodins for inspiring me to inquire.

Most important, I thank my mother, Gladys Goodin Tomlinson, for sparking my desire to persevere.

My special thanks go to Bertha H. McLaughlin for her patient processing of the manuscript and to Carolyn Faust for organizing the references.

INTRODUCTION

Postsecondary developmental programs designed to assist the underprepared college applicant have been in existence for much longer than is usually acknowledged. Divisions or departments currently labeled as "developmental studies" or "learning assistance" by institutions of higher education operate for the same basic purposes as services that were once known as "college preparatory." The presence and problems of underprepared students were recognized in some of the most prestigious institutions of higher learning as early as the 1860s, long before the enrollment of World War II veterans and the influx of students generated by desegregation.

This monograph describes the various perspectives on the evolution of developmental programs, their current modes of operation, their clients, and the issues surrounding their administration. The intent is to provide information that will help answer questions related to whether institutions of higher education should offer developmental programs for underprepared students, whether such involvement diminishes the academic integrity of the institution, and the extent to which institutions should be involved in such programs if they elect to offer developmental services.

The literature strongly suggests that the point of commitment to the implementation of developmental assistance is the trend in academic achievement scores over the past two decades—lost ground has not yet been fully recovered. In addition, issues of excellence versus equity, junior versus senior college administration of developmental programs, and the preparedness of program staff and administrators are prominent concerns among developmental educators, policymakers, and the general public. These problems are also explored.

The purpose, function, and nature of developmental programs are delineated in the report in order to illustrate the similarities that have existed for over a century. Specific definitions of developmental programs are taken from the literature to provide perspective on how the roles and functions of these programs have been viewed over the years. The variability of admission and placement standards established by colleges and universities, however, makes it impossible to arrive at a conclusive definition of developmental programs in terms of the concept of college-level work. Rationales for the existence, continuance, and expansion of these programs are emphasized in a discussion of social and technological changes as they apply to advanced age populations and young adults (Cross 1981), the level of underpreparedness among college freshmen (Hardesty 1986), and the popular conceptualizations of developmental services (H. Astin 1985; Gordon 1971).

Although the primary purpose of postsecondary learning assistance services at institutions of higher education has remained the same for more than a century, the content and scope of these services have changed. Whereas program focus was once limited to how-to-study techniques, basic reading, writing, and math skills improvement have been incorporated into the thrust of most developmental services by means of diagnosis, prescription, and tutorial assistance, which are accompanied by counseling and peer support to address attitudinal and self-management variables. The scope of services in any program may include classroom instruction, laboratory tutorials and self-paced activities, experiential activities on and off campus (e.g., plays, poetry readings, job training), and computer-monitored feedback on individual progress for students participating in the program.

Developmental courses have been offered at two-year, four-year, and university-level institutions, but it is frequently argued that academic assistance programs should be administered primarily at the junior-college level. Of the numerous developmental programs established at senior institutions, however, many have experienced successes and failures similar to those of programs at two-year institutions. Exemplary programs (e.g., the University of Minnesota's General College Retention Program and the Freshman Studies Program at Livingston College, Rutgers University) and the specific problems inherent to program operation are also presented.

The need for developmental programs that deliver instruction of the utmost integrity in terms of purpose, content, and scope is critical in efforts to optimize individual capabilities such that students are encouraged to feel that they can exert control over themselves and their environment through the enhancement of basic skills and the use of information that is classic, contemporary, and futuristic. Basic skills should be interrelated with and applied to content areas as well as areas of interest that auxiliary programs usually aim to address. Although statistics indicate that there are more courses offered in developmental mathematics across institutions, the realization that reading and writing are the basic skills more often necessary for daily survival has prompted a greater emphasis on reading and language arts concerns in this report.

Programs of honest intent and integrity can afford to make a sincere effort to imbue students with a sense of self-worth and integrity by acknowledging their cultures, philosophies, and milieus in all that the curriculum imparts. This report includes some program descriptions and philosophies that reflect such efforts. Commendable progress has been made in many instances, but there is still much room for the improvement and refinement of developmental programs in term of goals, objectives, and approaches.

Many changes in educational programs have occurred in the 1980s. There have been new commitments to excellence, new criteria for admission and placement, and new philosophies of instructional practice. Each of these changes is examined in the report in terms of the implications for developmental services. Particular attention is given to Sternberg's model for training intelligence, Feuerstein's program of instrumental enrichment, and Lipman's application of philosophy in the classroom—all of which are relevant to the possibilities for refining developmental instruction. These three instructional theories represent programs of training that have been widely implemented and successful in improving aspects of verbal comprehension, visual/spatial problem solving, and the logic of thought and expression.

The strength of the nation depends on our ability to equip the broadest spectrum of the population with the knowledge and skills that are required to face the increasing demands of global competition and the increasing demands of our immediate environments. Critical factors that will ultimately affect developmental programs are teacher training, funding, and the nature of assessment and evaluation processes at both the secondary and postsecondary levels. Educational institutions must meet these challenges at all levels, and for all who seek to participate.

HISTORICAL PERSPECTIVE OF POSTSECONDARY DEVELOPMENTAL EDUCATION

Programs designed for similar purposes as those we now know as "developmental studies" have been in existence in the United States for well over 100 years. Despite the variety of more recent labels for such programs (academic development, student support services, special studies, or student development), programs dubbed as "college preparatory" have existed since the mid-1800s to serve many of the same goals as today's programs. Historical accounts document this early evolution of developmental programs for the postsecondary student.

By 1907, more than 50 percent of the students entering Harvard, Yale, Columbia, and Princeton could not meet admission standards.

The presence of underprepared students in American colleges was recorded as early as the seventeenth century and has been attributed to a social structure in which wealth, more than ability, decided who went to college (Roberts 1986). The emergence of learning assistance programs for college-level study was officially ushered in by such events as the publication of the first how-to-study manual by Todd in 1836; the recognition of students' underpreparedness for university studies in English, a transition from the previous use of Latin in classrooms, which was highlighted by Henry P. Tappan in his inaugural presidential address at the University of Michigan in 1852; and by the signing of the Morrill Act of 1862, which established land-grant colleges and new purposes for higher education through agricultural and mechanical courses (Dempsey 1985). By the late nineteenth century, institutions such as Vassar College and Cornell University were experiencing problems with the academically deficient student (Roberts 1986).

Evolution of Developmental Programs in United States

A close look at the evolution of developmental programs in the United States reveals the following course of significant events and conditions. In 1865, the University of Wisconsin registered 331 students, of which only 41 were considered regular enrollees—the others were assigned to the "preparatory department" or classified as "special students" (Dunbar 1935). In 1866, the achievement levels of the first students at Vassar were described in the president's annual report to the board as a range of grade levels from a point appropriate for a college junior to a point lower than any scale used could indicate (Vassar College 1866). By 1872, a Preparatory Studies program was established at Vassar after discrepancies were noted between the popular ideal of elevating entrance requirements, to eliminate low student-achievement records at the college, and the president's philosophy that it would be financially more equitable to have underprepared students than no students at all (Roberts 1986). Preparatory enrollment students became 45 percent of the total student enrollment at Vassar by 1876, which led to great controversy. Faculty who taught preparatory students were stigmatized by those who taught the regular collegiate curriculum, and "subcollegiate" students were stigmatized by the regular students. A perception of Vassar as "half college and half academy" finally resulted in stronger ties with secondary schools regarding admission policies and the discontinuance of the Preparatory Studies program (Roberts 1986).

The common problem of the underprepared college student was reemphasized from an instructional perspective in publications emerging in 1877 and 1880 that focused on the nature of college reading, its demands, and the appropriate techniques (Dempsey 1985). There was also the simultaneous installment of the first freshman English course at Harvard in response to faculty complaints (Maxwell 1979).

The trend toward breaking the traditional mode of education that had prevailed in the seventeenth and eighteenth centuries was given additional momentum by the signing of the Morrill Act of 1890, which increased federal aid to higher education in applied sciences and mechanical art as a way to expand opportunities for postsecondary education for Americans (Maxwell 1979). In the same year, and at a time when many new institutions were competing for students, the College Entrance Examination Board was founded and given the mission of making college admission standards uniform (Dempsey 1985). Both of these events contributed to the increasing need for learning assistance.

By 1907, more than 50 percent of the students entering Harvard, Yale, Columbia, and Princeton could not meet admission standards, and by 1915 courses had been established to address underpreparedness at 350 colleges in the nation (Maxwell 1980). During the 1920s almost 100 books on study habits were written to accommodate the instructional needs of the emerging preparatory courses (Blake 1953). During this period also, scholarly research supported the need for postsecondary learning assistance programs (Albright 1927;

Book 1927; Remmers 1927), the first instrument to measure college reading achievement was published (Haggerty and Eurich 1929), and the first survey of remedial assistance programs was conducted (Parr 1930). In addition to the focus on study skills in the assistance programs, a predominant emphasis on reading instruction is attributed to the prevalence of freshman survey courses at the time, which required extensive reading (Dempsey 1985).

The 1930s saw continuous growth of the importance placed on reading improvement in academic assistance. The greatest strides were made in the diagnosis and categorization of reading deficiencies. The development of the tachistoscope as a mechanical aid in improving reading rate, the establishment of college and university reading clinics that served as teacher training and undergraduate learning assistance programs, the public schools' attention to remedial reading, and the emerging trend of using a battery of psychological, reading, vocabulary, physiological, and visual tests to determine abilities and deficiencies—all indicate the increased focus on reading. Also evident during this time was the growth of research on college students' reading abilities (Dempsey 1985), which provides a significant historical perspective (Buswell 1939; Robinson 1933). The majority of academic assistance programs, however, still focused on how-to-study courses developed primarily on the basis of narrowly perceived causes of underachievement, such as immaturity and poor study habits, commonly identified in students from "good families" (Cross 1976).

A significant increase in the addition of remedial reading to the how-to-study courses in academic assistance programs occurred during the 1940s. These new courses were characterized mainly as voluntary and noncredit and were conducted by counselors or other student personnel staff. Some institutions offered these courses in summer sessions as pre-freshman preparation. The increased focus on remedial reading is attributed to the depressed performance on standardized tests, which had gained popularity throughout the previous decade (Cross 1976).

An intensification in establishing remedial and developmental programs during the late 1950s and early 1960s is associated with an increased understanding of the nature and scope of the post-World War II college enrollment expansion, which was due in part to the flood of veterans entering college after the war. Valuable retrospective documentation of reading and study skills instruction is available in comprehensive research reports of the period (Blake 1953; Leedy 1958) that trace the development of materials, programs, and other relevant research and reports from 1900 to the late 1950s. Personal, demographic, and academic analyses illustrate the diverse dimensions of the new student populations. More attention was directed to psycho- and sociocultural factors of academic achievement, and remedial and developmental programs were considered essential to reduce the educational differences among students. The results of achievement tests and other measures enabled colleges to distinguish between "low-ability" students and "underachievers," and in response to those findings, counseling and motivational programs were developed to address academic achievement. This new focus and the expansion of programs were still not designed to meet the needs of those who fell into the "low-ability" category, and those students remained unable to persist in college programs (Cross 1976). Several surveys conducted during the 1960s reveal a comparatively low level of involvement in educating the disadvantaged in institutions of higher education (Egerton 1968; Simmons 1970). In a survey of 2,131 colleges and universities, for example, only 37 percent (224) of the responding institutions reported having compensatory programs—nearly one-half of which were serving fewer than 30 "new" (disadvantaged) students (Gordon and Wilkerson 1966).

The late 1960s and early 1970s were marked by massive college enrollments across the nation and greater efforts by institutions of higher education to meet the challenge of serving a fully diverse and pluralistic student body. Academic support programs began to address sociocultural differences and other variables that influence the development of the "low ability" student as well as the "underachiever." The "new" college entrants of this era were typically women, ethnic minorities, and those scoring in the lowest third of national samples on academic ability tests (Cross 1976, 1981). Major contributions to the literature on reading and study skills instruction were again produced in comprehensive reviews of surveys documenting program developments (Lowe 1966), of major trends in instruction (Lowe 1970), of specific periods of significance in the field (Ahrendt 1975; Leedy 1964), and of the specific focus on the development of one particular program type—the learning assistance model (Enright 1975). Surveys conducted at this time indicate a greater commitment to and involvement in special educational programs. Out of 180 midwestern community colleges, for example, 80 percent (110) offered remedial courses to prepare the "new" students for their regular curriculum, 50 percent (68) provided academic skills services, and almost 33 percent (47) had comprehensive programs incorporating tutorials, academic and nonacademic counseling, and remedial courses. In addition, one out of nine students at the responding institutions was involved in some sort of developmental education (Ferrin 1971). A survey of 337 predominantly white colleges and universities in the South indicated widespread involvement in such programs. When asked to describe innovative rather than traditional programs of remedial curriculum, 100 presidents reported 460 innovative programs at their institutions (Southern Regional Education Board 1971). Remedial education has been estimated to be one of the fastest growing areas of the college curriculum during the 1970s (Wright and Cahalan 1985).

The 1980s have seen further improvement in the design and implementation of programs to meet the needs of the underprepared. Institutions of higher education have become increasingly aware of the need for support services that can assist the underprepared student with personalized cognitive, social, and affective development as well as pragmatic, individualized, basic skills development (Cross 1976). Significant contributions to the professional literature preceding and during this period reflect an emphasis on general historical trends (Sanders 1979), specific trends in experimental research on college-level instruction in reading and study skills (Bailey 1982), and the evaluation of research on the effectiveness of college reading programs (Glass 1976)— all of which are undoubtedly useful in establishing and refining programs.

In sum, the evolution of academic assistance programs since the nineteenth century has been a progression from isolated, narrowly conceived, poorly funded efforts to integrated, broadly conceptualized, regularly budgeted programs (Roberts 1986). Along with progress in the development of these programs, however, there has also been resistance.

There has been much debate over whether remedial or basic skills courses should be offered at certain types of schools. The Illinois legislature, for example, passed a resolution in 1977 calling for the reduction of remedial courses at the university level and for the concentration of any necessary remedial courses at the community-college level by 1983. The Illinois resolution also supported the idea that degree credit should not be awarded for such courses. In 1984, the governor of Virginia called for higher admission standards as a way of reducing remedial programs, which he generally perceived as wasteful. Maryland administrators, indeed, instituted higher admission standards in the same year and experienced declines in remedial English enrollment. New Jersey administrators tried a different approach. They established a Basic Skills Council with the legal mandate to test all students' basic skills at the point of college entry and to encourage the requirement of remedial course work for all who were deficient. A priority mission of the council is to work with the high schools to intensify their focus on basic skills instruction. In 1983, for the first time since the inception of the program in 1977, the council reported a decrease in the percentage of college entrants found to be deficient in the basic skills areas tested (Wright and Cahalan 1985).

Remedial education and its relationship to equity are often perceived to be in conflict with the desire to maintain high standards and cost efficiency. The Commission on Excellence in Education holds that these goals should not be mutually exclusive, however.

Some of the controversy associated with remediation has been related to the variety of labels that schools across the country have placed on remedial courses. (Table 1 traces the labels used since the 1860s.) Labeling has been significant in that it is not only a product of remedial program organization, structure, and targeted groups, but also of public perception, state and university policy, and other factors (Wright and Cahalan 1985).

Labeling has also created difficulty in defining academic assistance programs for the underprepared. The remainder of this section delineates the purpose, function, and nature of these programs; provides generic definitions; and addresses the issue of variability in admission and placement procedures, which further complicates efforts to define these programs.

TABLE 1

LABELS USED FOR DEVELOPMENTAL PROGRAMS
AND THEIR STUDENT POPULATIONS FROM 1860
TO PRESENT

Time Span	Program Labels	Student Labels
1860s to 1890s	college preparatory preparatory studies	special students
1900s to 1940s	remedial assistance learning assistance how-to-study	underachievers unprepared students
1950s to present	developmental remedial compensatory special studies academic skills services basic skills college reading academic rehabilitation college study skills academic support learning assistance	low ability underachievers disadvantaged underprepared deficient high risk nontraditional

Purpose

The overall purpose of so-called college preparatory and developmental studies programs has been to eliminate academic deficiencies that diminish students' potential to succeed in college-level courses. More specifically, the purpose has been to assist the student in developing skills that would ensure success on entrance or proficiency exams or in meeting other admissions criteria.

Function

The function of these programs has primarily been to offer alternative programs of study to students who would have been denied admission to institutions of higher education by regular standards. The programs have most frequently been designed to prepare entering freshmen to meet the challenge of college-level courses in a variety of disciplines within the core course requirements. These services have usually been provided through a series of special courses, often for no credit, that allow the student to enroll in regular courses on successful completion of the preliminary program.

Nature

The nature of these offerings has been primarily remedial; the focus is on basic skills in reading, writing, and mathematics, and the application of those skills to content area materials. Many of these courses have used content area materials that progress in difficulty from secondary level to a level commensurate with that of materials used in the regular course offerings at the institution of higher education. A major emphasis in most of these programs has been study and test-taking strategies.

Definition and Ambiguities

There is much cross-usage of such terms as "remedial," "developmental," and "compensatory" in referring to programs that assist students in obtaining required levels of proficiency they have failed to meet. This cross-usage is a problem in the reality of program operations, as is the ambiguity of the phrase "college-level study" (see below). The term "remedial" denotes the correction of poor habits; the term "developmental" denotes that which is related to the effort to bring something into being as if for the first time; and the term "compensatory" denotes the provision of knowledge, abilities, or skills that will substitute for others that are required. The essence of each of these conditions, however, can often be found in programs that are labeled by any one of these terms when those programs are in the business of helping students to negotiate the regular postsecondary curriculum. (For example, in more unusual but increasing instances of learning-disabled students pursuing postsecondary education, services are delivered in a variety of manners and settings, from learning or remedial centers to specific programs designed for learning-disabled students.) In any of these settings, educators are called on to assist students in choices regarding remediation or compensation (Norlander and Anderson 1987). In practice, any program serving students at the postsecondary level who have failed to demonstrate required proficiencies may be involved in the delivery of services that encompass remedial, developmental, and compensatory approaches.

"Developmental education" is an umbrella term for a variety of instructional programs and individualized services that are unified by basic educational assumptions about variation of learning style being greater than ability to learn, variation of age for the achievement of educational potential, and the ability of those with varied cultural or environmental backgrounds or physical or economic handicaps to learn—given the appropriate conditions and strategies (Illinois Association for Personalized Learning Programs 1985). Thus, developmental studies programs have been defined from a variety of perspectives. This cross-usage is evident in Erickson and Rosica's (1978) definition of the course offerings of these programs:

The courses described as developmental range from remedial type reading courses, through basic writing, mathematics, science, and advanced study techniques. They generally cover all levels of academic achievement and consist of individualized, prescriptive laboratory experiences as well as large-group lecture approaches (p. 19).

Erickson and Rosica perceive developmental programs as learning or learner oriented. Christ (1971) supports this perception in his definition of learning centers:

A learning assistance center will be any place where learners, learning data, and learning facilitators are interwoven into a cybernetic, individualized, people oriented system to service all students (learners) and faculty (learning facilitators) of any institution where learning by its students is important (p. 3).

In a *Response to Findings of the Office for Civil Rights* the Regents Test Program of the University System of Georgia (1984) described its developmental studies program as one that exists to assist students in the elimination of academic deficiencies that prevent their full admission to collegiate-level courses. Developmental programs vary greatly in their specific purposes, goals, features, dimensions, and parameters within which they operate. Any one program may be in a constant state of change due to internal variables, such as characteristics of the student population, and external variables, such as institutional mission or state funding. A program that was labeled as a freshman seminar over 12 years ago at a college in the Northeast, for example, has evolved from a course in survival skills for high-risk freshmen showing deficiencies in mathematics, reading, and writing, with both voluntary and mandatory assignments in its first year; to a graduation requirement for all entering full-time, first-time freshmen in the next year, with academic credit; to a course moved from Student Affairs to Academic Affairs, with assigned rather than voluntary instructors and sections added for undeclared majors, three years later; to a course whose curriculum currently focuses on intellectual issues as well as advisory information, introduces liberal arts topics, and requires a written project. The seminar is said to have "evolved from a small program for freshmen deficient in basic skills, to a general orientation course, to a critical thinking seminar," and those shifts are said to reflect national trends (Dunphy, Miller, Woodruff, and Nelson 1989, p. 6).

From a success-ratio perspective, the most operational and pervasive definition indicates that the most successful developmental programs can be defined as multidimensional or holistic in the sense that they help students develop attitudes, skills, and values, thereby markedly improving success ratios for high-risk students. Thus, the most successful programs are those concerned with the education of the "whole student," that is, they emphasize development of the affective aspects of their clients (J. Roueche and Snow 1977).

From the perspective of placement standards, however, a recent Southern Regional Education Board (SREB) report indicates that, even within the parameters of a basic definition of developmental programs at the postsecondary level, there is very little consensus on what college-level work is (Abraham 1986). This lack of consensus is evident in the results of a study of college placement standards, specifically in terms of cutoff scores on placement tests (reading, writing, and mathematics), that was conducted in the SREB states—Alabama, Arkansas, Florida, Georgia, Kentucky, Louisiana, Maryland, Mississippi, North Carolina, Oklahoma, South Carolina, Tennessee, Texas, Virginia, and West Virginia. The regional survey found that, across these southeastern states, the term "college-level" varied greatly among two-year and four-year public institutions. "In fact, depending on the test selected, these data indicate that entry-level placement is based on scores that vary from as low as the 1st percentile to as high as the 94th percentile" (Abraham 1986, p. 4). A subsequent SREB study at the state or system level shows that there is also "little consensus for institutions in the same state and higher educational system on college-level placement standards" (Abraham 1987, p. 15).

In analyzing the data in that same study, Abraham found the following:

> *In every SREB state there is more than one means of determining college-level placement. The average number of placement tests used per state in the region is eight in reading, eight in mathematics, and seven in writing. The number of different placement tests used in any one curricula area range from as few as three in Georgia for mathematics to as many as 18 in North Carolina and Texas, also for mathematics* (p. 7).

Only three SREB states had statewide placement standards in 1987: Florida, Georgia, and Tennessee. Arkansas and Texas had a legislative mandate for developing such standards, and five other states were at some stage of considering a placement program. In most SREB states, colleges and universities have institutional autonomy to establish their own standards.

If variance exists within the three SREB states that have statewide standards, then it follows that the variance within states lacking statewide policy will be even greater. Thus, it is virtually impossible to arrive at a truly collective definition of developmental programs that could be considered representative of institutions of higher education in general. Very few global assumptions can be made about the standards, quality, or value of the undergraduate experience—even at the postsecondary developmental level.

THE RATIONALE FOR DEVELOPMENTAL PROGRAMS

In keeping with the emphasis on people-oriented, "whole student" definitions of successful developmental programs that pervade the literature, wherein students' attitudes as well as skills are addressed by faculty and staff, a student-focused approach is necessary in the delivery of services to students. Thus, it seems that the optimal efficiency in such endeavors would be contingent on sensitivity to what the individual student brings to the educational environment as well as what he or she may not have in common with the educational environment. Cultural background, social influences, and academic needs of the student should receive equal consideration in the development of instructional goals and practices. Since students enrolled in developmental programs are in conflict with traditional expectations of institutions of learning, some degree of compartmentalization inevitably exists between student and school. Where students are usually limited in the time allowed for fulfillment of standard requirements, programs that seek to close the gaps should avoid a compartmentalized approach to instruction. In sum, the most effective developmental programs may well be defined as those that address the whole student and present a whole (interdisciplinary) academic process to the student.

The most effective developmental programs may well be defined as those that address the whole student and present a whole academic process to the student.

Despite the long-standing history of learning assistance services, questions regarding the rationale for developmental programs, their purpose, and their place are frequently posed. Some of the most provocative questions have been expressed as follows:

- What should be the role of the institutions of higher education in regard to the underprepared student?
- Should universities admit students who are not adequately prepared for college?
- Should colleges and universities engage in providing academic preparation for the academically underprepared student?
- Should institutions of higher education offer academic work considered to be on a precollegiate level? (Roberts 1986, p. 1)

Observable and projected changes in the diversity of levels of preparedness of high school graduates, sociological and technological change, and employment trends and other demographic factors create educational needs that affect the role and responsibility of institutions of higher education.

The New and Diverse Target Population

The characteristics and needs of the target groups for services now known as developmental studies have come to reflect the new diversity of the student population at the postsecondary level. A change in philosophy regarding the purpose of a college education has, in turn, created a change in the numbers of minorities and individuals of low socioeconomic status who pursue their fundamental right to postsecondary education. Consequently, there has also been an increase in the number of educationally disadvantaged—and under-prepared—individuals who seek enrollment in institutions of higher education.

Cross's (1981) discussion of the more advanced age population seeking postsecondary education has implications for young adults who are of traditional school age. Aside from demographic factors resulting in larger numbers of adults in the total population, Cross also addresses the influences of social change and technological change. Social change, characterized by "the rising educational level of the populace, the changing roles of women, early retirement, civil rights, increased leisure time, and changing life-styles," has caused education for adults to become "necessary for some, desirable for others, and more acceptable and attainable for almost everyone" (p. 3). Technological change, according to Cross, has created a situation in which "almost any worker in the society has the problem of keeping up with new knowledge and of adapting to technological change as consumers as well as producers" (p. 3). This new trend for advanced age groups has also influenced the circumstances, if not the perceptions, of the younger generation with respect to the value of a higher education as it relates to increased numbers of individuals competing in the labor force.

Although the growth in population in the age range of 15 to 29 years will decrease through at least 2000, the unemployment rate for young minority group members and the educationally disadvantaged is predicted to increase drastically. Thus, there will still be a considerable influx of the "new clientele" pursuing enrollment in institutions of higher education. Postsecondary education has become at least a bastion, if not a necessity, for those who anticipate difficulty in obtaining gainful and meaningful employment. Another reason for an increase of "new clientele" is that those who are fortunate enough to find "meaningful employment" on graduation from high school enter postsecondary institutions in the years ahead. What may seem to be meaningful employment for high school seniors may seem less meaningful with experience and time. Thus, more individuals will seek reentry into the educational system—still in need of academic development in order to gain admission at the postsecondary level.

According to a report of the Special Studies Program of the University System of Georgia (1984), "the size and importance of this problem began to appear to many people in the University System in the mid-sixties. [It was] not fully perceived, but there was each year a growing conception of a larger and more serious problem" (p. 64). The target group has been characterized as consisting mainly of incoming freshmen who fail to meet regular admissions criteria, are admitted provisionally, and are usually classified as high-risk students (J. Roueche and Snow 1977).

More recently, Hardesty (1986) of the Coordinating Board of the Texas College and University System made the following statement:

At least 30,000 freshmen who enter Texas public colleges and universities each year cannot read, write or compute at levels needed to perform effectively in higher education. . . . The committee's report shows that students who meet the standard admission criteria at the state's public colleges still lack basic skills. . . . They are intelligent, qualified students, competent enough to meet entrance requirements despite a deficiency in given skills. To prevent them from entering college would bar too many capable students from higher education (p. 1).

A recent Southern Regional Education Board report indicates that findings in the 15 southeastern member states are consistent with other state and national studies on the numbers of students entering college who are not ready to do college-level work. The report states that "36 percent—close to four of ten—first-time entering college freshmen need additional academic support in reading, writing, or mathematics" (Abraham 1988, p. 2).

Projections
Enrollment in developmental programs has clearly increased in recent years, and it is likely to continue to increase into

the 1990s. It is predicted that a part of this increase will result from increased recruitment of disadvantaged students. According to demographic trends, there will be more white students from rural areas, more suburban students, and more low-income students from suburban areas (Boylan 1985).

This new diversity has necessitated the restructuring of programs to meet the needs of clients. The new population of applicants is increasing more rapidly than the rate at which high school curriculum and teacher preparation for secondary schools can possibly change. Thus, many theorists indicate that developmental studies programs should be considered an integral facet of higher education. A. Astin (1975) supports this notion in the following statement:

> *A number of mechanisms are available to most institutions [of higher education] to bring about greater student participation: academic programs, admissions, freshmen orientation, counseling and advisement, financial aid, work opportunities, extra-curricular activities, and housing and student services . . . The possible intervention techniques are numerous: tutoring, programmed instruction, special courses for developing study skills, and self-paced learning among others. Institutions can, with relatively little investment of resources, carry out controlled experiments on a limited scale to identify the most promising approaches: with well designed studies, the more effective techniques in raising student's performance can be identified within a short time—say, within one term after initiating the study* (p. 45).

Moreover, it would seem that senior institutions of higher education would be most adequately equipped to provide successful programs of academic development. These institutions house schools of education with faculty and graduate students specializing in the critical areas of developmental/ remedial instruction and counseling. Growth trends reflect that, prior to 1960, the highest percentage of such programs were found at institutions offering postgraduate instruction. Again, by 1976 there was increased involvement of senior colleges and universities in the provision of remedial and developmental services (J. Roueche and Snow 1977). These senior institutions are usually committed to community service projects, which often establish viable links to the public schools, where in-service training/staff development can do much to inform all individuals, secondary and postsecondary, who are concerned with meeting the needs of the target populations.

Currently, developmental/remedial or academic support programs hold vast potential in the movement toward equal educational opportunity in a democratic society. One of the traditional roles of education in the United States has been to broaden opportunities for productive, influential and rewarding participation in the affairs of society by developing the skills and credentials necessary for economic and social satisfaction (Gordon 1971). A recent increase in required educational competency levels is reflected in the 10-year College Board Educational Equality Project (1983), in the new criteria implemented by the Southern Association of Colleges and Schools in 1988, and in the higher Scholastic Aptitude Test (SAT) score requirements for many institutions of higher education. At a time when high school graduation and college entrance requirements are being made more stringent nationwide, there will still be numbers of hopeful students who will not meet the admissions criteria. Gordon's (1971) discussion of the purpose of education in a democratic society illuminates the critical role of developmental programs for those who fall short of standard college entrance requirements:

> If that purpose [of education in a democratic society] is to broaden opportunities for meaningful participation in the mainstream of society . . . then educational opportunity is unequal unless it serves that purpose for all learners. At any point in the history of a society, the minimum educational goals are defined by the prerequisites for meaningful participation or for economic, social and political survival. The educational experience can and should enable many persons to go far beyond the development of such survival skills but it cannot be considered to have provided equality of opportunity unless it enables nearly all [save the 3% to 5% who are truly mentally defective] to reach the survival or participation level (p. 7).

If college admission criteria will exclude some high school graduates, then developmental studies programs can continue to play a critical role in the scheme of higher education by

providing the kind of instruction and preparation that some individuals need in order to gain access to postsecondary educational experience.

Arguments on Role and Responsibility

Although senior institutions of higher education traditionally have more resources, facilities, and scholars and researchers with the acumen to address the needs of the underprepared student, many individuals hold that developmental courses are best suited to two-year community colleges and should be excluded from four-year colleges and universities. This controversy has been put into perspective by Ross and Roe (1986), who indicate that every institution has its lowest students, many of whom need remediation. They refer to programs for underprepared students at Duke University, Ohio State University, Massachusetts Institute of Technology, and Stanford University. In reference to Harvard's remedial reading program, they quote William Perry (1959), who stated that "Harvard's 'remedial' students already were reading better than 85% of the nation's college freshmen, but they still needed help to measure up to the demands of their coursework" (p. 194).

In defense of the average student, it has been claimed that 95 percent can learn a subject to a high level of mastery if given sufficient learning time and appropriate types of help (Bloom 1971). Although it is predicted that a good remedial program can help only 50 percent of its students to perform adequately in regular courses and only 25 percent to meet graduation requirements (Moore, 1984), this success ratio is substantial given that many underprepared students suffer several years' deficiency in specific skills when they enroll in postsecondary developmental programs, which generally only allow one year of remediation.

Two interesting arguments are presented in defense of developmental programs in terms of role and responsibility. First, popular opinion often holds that developmental programs dilute academic programs, but proponents of developmental programs argue that their role is to support and enrich the regular curriculum and ensure that more students will succeed. From this perspective, remedial courses are viewed as additions to, not replacements for, the required courses in a student's program of study (Ross and Roe 1986).

Second, it is often argued that many of the skills taught

in developmental education programs at institutions of higher
education should have been mastered by the student earlier,
but that has not always been possible, for a variety of reasons.
Roberts (1986) concludes the following:

> It is impractical to expect adults to return to primary or
> secondary school to acquire the skills they need to be of
> value to themselves and to society. A choice must be made.
> Developmental education programs demonstrate that society
> has decided to help individuals overcome their skill defi-
> ciencies. The alternative would be to allow those individuals
> to remain a liability not only to themselves but also perhaps
> to society as well (p. 71).

Learning Deficiencies

Underprepared students may exhibit any of a great variety
of learning deficiencies, but they most often fall into the basic
categories of reading, writing, mathematics, and study skills.
In the area of reading, underprepared students often lack adequate skills in regard to vocabulary, word decoding (phonics),
text comprehension, and reading rate. In the writing category,
the most prevalent skill deficiencies of the underprepared
learner are usually found in sentence and paragraph construc-
tion, grammatical coherence within sentences and paragraphs,
logical and sequential structure of compositions and essays,
and spelling. In mathematics, many underprepared students
lack necessary computational skills and are deficient in understanding fundamental mathematical concepts; many suffer
mainly from "math phobias."

From a cognitive perspective, underprepared students are
often found to function at a literal thinking level (used for
memory, translation, and interpretation in reading) and are
unfamiliar with higher thinking levels (used for analysis, syn-
thesis, and evaluation in reading) and/or abstract thinking
(often required in problem solving). Research has suggested
that more than 50 percent of college freshmen may not be
at Piaget's formal operational level of thinking (Ross and Roe
1986).

In the area of study skills, often considered a sub-skill of
reading proficiency for higher learning, and inclusive of self-
management, underprepared students are usually lacking
in an adequate repertoire of study strategies for texts in the
content areas, novels, and other literature; listening, note-
taking, and test-taking strategies; and time management skills.

Experiential Deficiencies

Lack of exposure to people, places, events, customs, and mundane features of life beyond the commonplace of an individual's immediate locale results in experiential deficiencies that are often debilitating to academic motivation or to the capacity for independent learning. Much of what would be considered new knowledge for the learner can only be acquired and synthesized through the use of a base of prior knowledge. Effective assimilation of new material depends greatly on an individual's storehouse of knowledge to which new information can be related.

The underprepared student is often one who may have the basic intellectual capacity but who has reached a point of impasse temporarily created by a mismatch between his or her knowledge base and the new information that he or she is expected to absorb on an independent basis. Experiential deficiencies combined with the specific learning deficiencies described above can create serious disadvantages for the student. These circumstances of underpreparedness can be remediated, however.

Standardized Placement
Trends—SAT Averages

The College Board's 1986 *Admissions Testing Program National Report* on college-bound seniors indicates that from 1967 to 1986 SAT score averages have suffered an overall decline. Although there have been yearly increases in average scores on the verbal and math sections of the SAT recently, those increases have only brought the averages back to a level equal to the 1976 figures. In 1967, the total mean verbal score for males and females was 466; in 1976, 431; and after a continuous drop from 1967 to 1980, the mean has increased steadily to a score of 431 in 1986—still 35 points below the 1967 average score. Math scores reveal the same trend. In 1967, the mean math score was 492 for males and females; in 1976, 472; and after the same downtrend as verbal scores from 1967 to 1980, the mean math score has increased since 1980 to 475 in 1986—still 17 points below the 1967 score.

The profile provided by SAT scores is not representative of all high school graduates nor all college freshmen, but it is representative of a substantial national sample of approximately two-fifths of all high school graduates—approximately 890,000 students. It is obvious that there has been a decline in achievement scores over the past two decades that has not yet been remedied. Because the strength of the nation depends on its ability to equip the broadest spectrum of its population with the knowledge and skills required to face the increasing demands of global competition, educational institutions must meet this challenge at all levels and for all who seek participation.

CHARACTERISTICS OF POSTSECONDARY DEVELOPMENTAL PROGRAMS

Of the numerous types of postsecondary developmental programs that exist (see descriptions in Ross and Roe 1986; Sharma 1977; Wright and Cahalan 1985), all have many features or services in common but each operates on the basis of some unique characteristic—most often resulting from the unique needs of its student population. Types of programs are discussed in this section in terms of types of student deficiencies usually addressed, services provided for the student, and the auspices under which the services are provided. Four types of programs predominate: college campus tutorial/remedial, college outreach programs, campus assistance centers, and off-campus instruction.

College campus tutorial/remedial programs are campus based and usually offered to students as noncredit courses; some tutorials are provided on a nonmandatory basis to lend academic support to high-risk students who may be enrolled in credit courses. Such programs also often include financial assistance, counseling, and in some cases, special educational services to help upgrade the academic skills of disadvantaged students. This category also includes a unique alternative known as the grade deletion policy program, which is designed to help students find a more appropriate choice of major if one is giving them considerable difficulty.

College outreach programs are usually conducted under affiliation with student community services. These programs provide such services as contacting prospective students, presenting information on college programs, and enrolling students in starter courses in conjunction with individual counseling; creating "highly cohesive and supportive" student organizations with special personnel and programs for specific minority ethnic groups, such as African-Americans, Chicanos, and Native Americans; providing continuing admission for students who succeed in special summer programs; providing Big Sisters/Brothers to help freshmen of minority ethnic groups; producing cultural festivals; and establishing satellite counseling centers in neighborhoods populated by university students characterized as alienated and hostile toward the "establishment." A unique service under this category of programs is the establishment of day-care centers for the children of students who are disadvantaged.

Campus assistance centers are those programs that are established to facilitate "communiversity" life. These programs

In most developmental programs that provide remediation in the basic skill areas, diagnostic processing is often an integral component.

provide such services as crisis intervention, student advocates, change agents, informational resources, and referral agencies. A unique service in this category is the "commuter affairs" program, which makes units of the campus physical plant available to commuting students for study, rest, and other between-class needs.

Off-campus programs of instruction are offered on the job, at home, and in other settings. Such programs provide educational opportunities and in-service learning projects outside the traditional classroom.

At first glance, some aspects of the program categories listed above may seem to be outside the boundaries of what are commonly perceived to be developmental studies programs. If one considers the most comprehensive definition of such programs and aims to address the whole student, however, it is evident that a conscientious combination of the above-mentioned services would, in most cases, be in the best interest of those who are most typically in need of provisional admission to institutions of higher education. Other labels for the identification of similar services include special studies programs, learning assistance centers, course-related learning services, and comprehensive learning systems (see table 1 for additional program descriptors). In most developmental programs that provide remediation in the basic skills areas, diagnostic processing is often an integral component of the program or the diagnostic services of another testing center or office on the campus are incorporated as a primary phase in the delivery of program services.

National estimates indicate that about 90 percent of all institutions of higher education have at least some of the services described above. About 33 percent report having a separate department or division for developmental studies or college learning centers. By type of school, the percentage having separately administered programs is as follows: public institutions, 47 percent; two-year, 43 percent; and open admission colleges and universities, 45 percent. Smaller institutions incorporate developmental services into their various academic departments (Wright and Cahalan 1985).

The same survey indicates that 24 percent of all institutions have a special pre-admission summer program that provides additional services to accompany basic remedial course work. Four-year traditional and selective schools are found to offer this type of program more frequently than two-year and open admission schools. Still, only about 33 percent of traditional and selective schools reported having such a program. In addition to the more popular basic skills courses in reading, writing, and mathematics, 58 percent of all institutions offer remedial courses in student development, and 21 percent offer remedial academic courses outside the three basic skills areas.

Thirty percent of the national population in higher education is involved in some form of developmental education, and in some southern institutions that figure is closer to 40 percent (Joiner 1988). In Georgia, for example, which is one of only a few states that have mandatory developmental programs, 30 to 40 percent of freshmen are required to enroll in at least one developmental studies area. This statistic is said to compare favorably with other states, such as Tennessee, half of whose freshmen need developmental work (Morgan 1988).

Alternative Structures

Early and midterm intervention programs have been operated in some institutions for students who are at risk in regular courses. Students receive tutoring in course content, extra instruction in laboratories, and counseling, all in lieu of enrollment in an actual developmental program (Ross and Roe 1986).

Another innovative type of developmental assistance is administered in the form of adjunct courses that are offered for high-risk courses, particularly at the introductory level, in areas such as social sciences, mathematics, the physical sciences, and the humanities. This approach coordinates two courses whereby a subject course taught by a regular faculty member is matched with an adjunct skills class taught by a learning skills instructor. Such a program has been implemented and found effective at the University of Missouri-Kansas City (Friedlander 1984).

The greatest departure from the traditional types of developmental programs can be found in the junior colleges, where the needs of the student population are different from those of students at senior colleges and universities. Four basic types of programs have been designed to help junior college students compensate for specific deficiencies. These programs are commonly known as pretransfer, adult basic education, handicapped, and remedial.

The pretransfer program in junior colleges is designed to

address deficiencies in grades or subjects required for admission to a senior institution, college, or transfer program. The adult basic education program addresses deficiencies in literacy and basic skills subjects necessary for a high school diploma. The handicapped programs address physical and mental handicaps that impose limitations on those students who are also academically or socially handicapped. Finally, the remedial programs are designed to address the same types of basic skills deficiencies and deficiencies in study strategies and self-management that are typically addressed in other developmental/remedial programs (Lombardi 1979).

Types of Interventions

For purposes of this discussion, types of intervention are distinguished from types of programs in that program descriptions indicate which services are offered, and types of intervention indicate the manner in which those services are provided and their affective intent. Types of intervention are categorized here as teaching/learning, counseling, peer support, and supplemental use of media and the arts.

Teaching/learning interventions are traditionally implemented through a variety of course offerings. The most prevalent structure of such interventions has been a program of courses divided into English (writing), reading, and math components.

From a national sample of 511 colleges and universities, the Higher Education General Information Survey enrollment report (Broyles 1982) indicated that 82 percent of the schools had at least one remedial/developmental course and that more colleges offered courses in remedial writing (73 percent) and mathematics (71 percent) than in reading (66 percent). In the majority of schools offering remedial programs, the courses are required if the student does not meet certain standards. Remedial writing courses are mandatory in about 64 percent, and remedial mathematics in about 59 percent, of schools offering the courses. Remedial reading courses are mandatory in about 51 percent of the schools offering the course (Wright and Cahalan 1985).

Examples of the more innovative interventions have been those related to human development and life-style, with a focus on the concerns of marginal students; introspection, with an emphasis on the experience of the student, leading to the evaluation of values, attitudes, beliefs, abilities, and relationships with others; community involvement; creative work; wilderness experiences; a focus on the interface of various disciplines; sensitization of administrators and faculty to the operation and philosophy of the program; and finally, tutorial/remedial application, which is most often provided as a supplement to the required course of study.

Counseling interventions, provided in the form of group or one-on-one interactions, address issues of values, attitudes, and human relationships development for students and faculty/staff, as well as personalized evaluation of academic progress to identify interests, abilities, and limitations. Case studies of programs at 19 institutions during the 1969-70 academic year indicated that tutoring, counseling and guidance services, and work-study opportunities were then common to many programs (H. Astin, Bisconti, and Frankel 1972). This programming trend remains prevalent today.

The most innovative type of counseling intervention described in the literature is the use of "dual function personnel," that is, tutors who are trained to perform counseling services in some of the following areas: building rapport, establishing credibility, assessing student needs and prescribing specific interventions, maintaining a task-oriented atmosphere, informing students of expectations in the teaching-learning relationship and the rest of the program, providing and eliciting feedback, providing positive reinforcement, and monitoring the progress of work. This type of intervention has been used successfully at the University of Southern California, where peer tutors/counselors are trained for these responsibilities (Jones 1984).

When this skills-therapy approach is used in the remedial program, the tutor/counselor must conduct in-depth interviews and diagnosis "to discover whether the academic problems are a cause or result of personal problems which may include escape and avoidance defenses, unrealistic goals, or inadequate self-concept" (Schmelzer and Brozo 1982, p. 647). Skills-therapy personnel do not have to be licensed counselors, but they should have strong backgrounds in psychology and counseling. This requisite combination of expertise makes it more difficult to staff a program initially, but it can be worthwhile in terms of the long-term effectiveness of the program (Ross and Roe 1986).

Peer support interventions have included peer tutoring, "buddy" systems, and a unique project in which emphasizing and monitoring student concerns, such as academic improvement, social contact, weight control, and class participation, are critical goals.

The media and the arts have been used to supplement the content of course work, tutorials, and counseling. An infinite variety of computer-assisted instructional services (Tomlinson 1987), for example, are made available in learning labs. Computerized monitoring systems are used in many developmental programs to track academic performance, effort, and attendance. Special handbooks have been published and distributed (1) to inform students from special interest groups about academic and social conditions on campuses and about national achievements and organizations related to their social interest and (2) to transmit such information to other students on campus for the purpose of discussion and the enhancement of image and confidence. Field trips have been conducted to engage students in the appreciation of dance, drama, and poetry related to special interest groups and various themes.

Modes of Delivery for Developmental Services

The delivery of developmental instruction is usually accomplished through the use of the traditional classroom, the laboratory approach, or a combination of both. In the classroom approach the instructor and students meet regularly several times a week to cover material and related strategies that are predetermined by a course outline or syllabus. In the laboratory approach the instructor and student may or may not meet on a regular basis, students may be allowed to develop their own schedules, or students may attend sporadically and infrequently if they have no mandatory lab appointments.

There are some disadvantages to both approaches to developmental instruction. In the classroom, students who are deficient in only some of the predetermined instructional sequence will inevitably spend some of the allotted course time receiving instruction they do not need. In the laboratory, when students attend at their convenience and have no prescribed assignments to address their deficiencies, they often seek assistance on immediate problems generated by course work and, thus, only do work to resolve immediate problems (Ross and Roe 1986).

Whether instruction is conducted in the classroom or the

laboratory, group size is critical. Group size should be low, particularly in a classroom setting, where 15 to 20 students is the desirable number and classes larger than 20 become unmanageable for individual instruction.

Operational Models

There are numerous developmental/remedial programs in existence but very few variations in basic program models. The most common type, tutorial/remedial programs, have evolved from either the developmental/remedial or holistic vs. skills-based philosophies (see following section). Some programs seek to assist students in obtaining proficiency in the basic skills and study skills necessary for success in college-level courses by tracking them through a series of courses in each basic skill area (reading, writing, mathematics) for which deficiencies have been identified. These courses are most often taught under separate subject components within a department for developmental/remedial services. Course content is usually based solely on the specific subject area. Students are usually given a set period of time in which to demonstrate proficiency in each area.

An alternative approach to traditional developmental/remedial instruction is the interdisciplinary structure within which the various basic skills courses are conducted in conjunction with each other. The reading class, for example, incorporates several writing assignments and math word problems, and the writing class uses reading course materials or topics as a springboard for discussion and essay assignments.

Some programs operate on the premise of a holistic model of instruction, which seeks to address remediation of the student's deficiencies by means of whole contexts (entire chapters, articles, books) and the use of global communication processes (reading for understanding, discussion, and written summaries or essay responses). Other programs incorporate a skills-based approach, which seeks to remediate the student's deficiencies through task analysis of the specific skills required to master assignments in a given subject area and individually prescribed assignments for practice of those individual skills in application to the course content and supplementary materials.

Group vs. individualized instruction has often evolved out of the holistic vs. skills-based approaches. Group instruction facilitates the holistic approach and is most often used for course offerings in a classroom setting with a lecture or seminar format. Group instruction has also been used in laboratory settings, where individualized instruction is used as well (Tomlinson 1985). Individualized instruction is seldom found in the classroom setting, due to class size and time constraints; it is more often used in laboratory settings to facilitate both holistic and skills-based approaches.

Laboratory instruction has been incorporated into many programs as a means of providing tutorial support for course work in the subject or skills area classes. Students are often scheduled into labs on a mandatory basis, in addition to the course schedule, and individualized education plans are prescribed as a supplement to course work. Labs have also served the ancillary function of providing impromptu tutoring for those students seeking assistance on a voluntary basis. Labs frequently accommodate the self-paced approach when instruction is individualized.

The majority of developmental/remedial programs have used combinations of these various approaches to deliver instructional services in the three basic skills areas (reading, writing, and mathematics) and have also incorporated a counseling component to provide additional support services. Students are assigned to counselors, who are available for advice on personal, academic, or social matters and who are often involved in relaying periodic progress reports from instructors to students.

Grading

Grading systems vary from campus to campus for developmental programs. Some institutions hold the philosophy that grades are threatening to the insecure remedial student and suggest either giving no grades or at least no failing grades as alternatives to the traditional grading system of letter grades. In these alternative cases, students would receive A's or B's for passing work, and those who fail would receive no grade. Other institutions are opposed to lenient grading policies and maintain that developmental grading policies should remain parallel to those of the rest of the institution. As another alternative, mastery learning is suggested such that students are allowed as much time as they need to remediate deficiencies (Ross and Roe 1986) to the point of passing.

More than half of the existing developmental programs give traditional letter grades and about 40 percent give nonstandard grades, such as pass/fail (J. Roueche, Baker, and S. Roueche 1984). The relevance of traditional grading practices has been questioned in application to developmental programs, and it has been suggested that assessment of academic success be made in terms of changes in an individual student's performance (A. Astin 1971).

Course Credit

Approximately 70 percent of those institutions who offer remedial courses do not give degree credit for such courses. The most common type of credit given for these courses is institutional credit, which determines the student's enrollment status and is recorded on the student's transcript, but does not accrue toward degree or certificate completion. Just over 50 percent of institutions report using this type of credit for remedial reading, writing, and mathematics. For the various alternative types of credit awarded, frequencies are as follows for writing (and very similar for reading and mathematics): institutional credit, 53 percent; elective credit, 25 percent; subject degree credit, 6 percent; and no formal credit, 16 percent (Wright and Cahalan 1985). (Some of the more non-traditional developmental courses outside the basic skills area may award credit differently.)

The awarding of credit may very well be a critical factor in the success ratios of students enrolled in developmental programs. S. Roueche (1983) indicates that research shows significant success for students in remedial courses giving credit, due to increased motivation. Many traditional institutions, however, would view this approach as a lowering of college standards (Wright and Cahalan 1985) and a lowering of the integrity of the institution's program by accepting precollegiate work on the same basis as collegiate work (Ross and Roe 1986). On the other hand, awarding no credit at all for student's efforts in remedial course work could be counterproductive—"demoralizing" to the student.

It seems that the awarding of institutional credit for developmental course work is the most popular compromise to the student motivation/institutional integrity dilemma. In addition to increasing student commitment, proponents indicate that institutional credit also enables students to qualify for veteran's benefits, athletic grants, and other forms of financial aid and provides a basis for determining faculty load and formula funding for the institutional budget.

Exit Criteria

Like grading and credit policies, the policy for exit criteria
also varies across institutions. Exit criteria determine the levels
of proficiency that a student must demonstrate and the time
frame within which the student must meet those predetermined competencies. For example, in a subject area such
as reading, students may be required to obtain a specified
course average, final exam score, and systemwide (regents)
competency test score minimums in order to exit the reading
course. In addition, where students may fail a first attempt
at meeting the exit criteria, a limited number of attempts are
allowed in a given subject such that anywhere from two to
four terms may be the limit for attempts to demonstrate proficiency and eligibility to exit the subject area.

In keeping with the mastery learning concept, advocates
emphasize the flexibility of an open entry/open exit policy,
which allows students to enter and leave developmental
courses according to their own rates of learning. Some programs allow students to "test out" of courses when they
believe they have met the objectives. From a practical perspective, time limits for exit are advisable. Where two terms
for a course is considered a reasonable limit, students who
fail two attempts may be prohibited from taking the course
for a consecutive third time, receive counseling for setting
alternative academic goals, be allowed to reenter the course
after a specified number of terms elapses, or under extreme
circumstances, be allowed to appeal the decision (Ross and
Roe 1986).

The Role of Junior and Senior
Colleges and Universities

Much of public opinion has maintained the notion that developmental programs should be administered exclusively by
the junior, two-year, colleges. Although historical accounts
and current statistics indicate that developmental services,
by any name, have been firmly established at junior and senior
colleges and universities, public and private, of every caliber,
a substantial part of the literature is devoted to the role of
community colleges in the delivery of developmental services
(Campbell 1982; Kerstiens 1971; Moore 1971; Roberts 1986;
J. Roueche 1984). (The terms junior college and community
college are used interchangeably in this discussion. Although
popularly used to denote "private academic two-year insti-

tution," the term "junior college" has not always been confined to this single usage. Until very recently, for example, public two-year colleges in Georgia that were not strictly academic carried the label "junior.")

The distribution of services reported in a 1985 survey (Wright and Cahalan) shows remedial courses offered at 88 percent of two-year and 78 percent of four-year institutions; 94 percent of public and 70 percent of private schools; and 91 percent of open and 68 percent of selective admissions institutions. The distribution of courses in a given subject was found to be typically one or two courses. Only about 10 percent of the colleges offered four or more remedial courses in a subject, and public, two-year, and open admission schools offered about one more course per subject than private, four-year, and selective schools.

The same survey shows the following distribution of the frequency of student enrollment in remedial work: 28 percent of freshmen in two-year colleges and 19 percent in four-year schools; 27 percent of freshmen in public colleges and 15 percent in private colleges; and 30 percent of freshmen in open colleges and 13 percent in selective and traditional admission colleges. The data indicate that remedial students are more likely to attend two-year, public, and open admission colleges. It should be noted that almost two-thirds of all first-year students enroll in two-year and open admissions colleges and 85 percent of all first-year students attend public colleges. Perhaps what appears to be a prevalence of developmental programs in two-year colleges is, to a great extent, a function of the nature of enrollment policy and trends rather than the efficacy or capability of two-year schools to provide developmental services.

Proponents of the idea that developmental programs are best suited to the junior college are, no doubt, inclined to see a definite link between the mission of the two-year school and the purpose of developmental course work. The two-year institution emerged in the early 1900s with an open door policy and the purpose of providing the disadvantaged high school graduate and the minority student an opportunity to transcend their socioeconomic status by improving their skills and gaining access to meaningful career opportunities (Bass 1982). Many of the courses taught in the junior college were designed to create equity in higher education, promote its popularity, and make education available to the public in general. The courses were created to address the needs of the following types of nontraditional students: the part-time student, the adult seeking refresher courses, the senior citizen, the handicapped veteran, the unemployed career changers, and the housewife entering the work force (Roberts 1986).

Junior colleges do have decades of experience in providing developmental or remedial education for underprepared students. By 1965, but before the widespread realization of desegregation in institutions of higher education, over 60 percent of the community college students ranked at or below the 30th percentile on the School and College Ability Test (Moore 1971). By the late 1960s the most frequently offered courses in community colleges were remedial reading, remedial writing, and remedial arithmetic (J. Roueche 1984).

Although junior colleges have historically fulfilled a mission that has consistently answered the needs of remedial students, they have often experienced the same problems in their efforts to deliver remedial services as have other types of institutions. In a survey of members of the American Association of Community and Junior Colleges (Campbell 1982), particular attention was given to Monroe County Community College, which was described as an institution that had been concerned about students with academic deficiencies since its founding in 1964 but had been unsuccessful in meeting the challenge. The extent of the institution's failure was evidenced by a discontinuation of remedial courses, due to lack of enrollment five years after opening; discontinuation of diagnostic testing for counseling and class placement, due to concerns that an older student population was reluctant to take the tests; concerns about grade inflation masking the need for remedial education; concerns about the validity of granting college credit for below college-level work; and the increasing costs of remedial/developmental courses. These concerns prompted the college to conduct the nationwide survey at a time when their own capacity to re-establish developmental services had improved.

Campbell reports that, at the time of the survey in 1981, out of 903 junior colleges, 98 percent offered remedial/developmental courses, 81 percent awarded credit for remedial course work—48 percent granted regular college credit. Thirty-eight percent thought that remedial courses should be offered for credit but not apply to transfer, and 16 percent thought that no credit should be awarded for remedial work.

The dilemmas experienced by Monroe County Community College and the responses to their national survey are representative of the problems and perspectives of many institutions of higher education, junior, senior, and university level, in responding to the challenge of delivering developmental services.

Numerous contributions to the literature on developmental programs specifically address the role of community colleges in such services. Although some of the issues or approaches that are discussed may appear to be unique to the junior college program, the majority of issues—particularly curriculum concepts—are applicable to any type of institution. The literature notes, for example, the following parameters in remediation at the junior college level: the use of both descriptive and prescriptive approaches to designing programs (Herscher 1980); offering compensatory programs and services as electives; requiring certain students to participate in skills courses; offering basic skills instruction as part of regular courses (Friedlander 1981); and support of the vital role of speech communication (Miller 1984).

From a practical perspective, additional arguments for a developmental program at every institution are presented in terms of access and transferability. Supporters of the idea that developmental programs should be maintained at every level of complex systems of higher education indicate that, if developmental programs are relegated to two-year colleges, then in cities that have senior colleges but no junior college, access would be denied to those students who are not within reach of a two-year college. In terms of transferability, those who support the idea of a program at every institution argue that a developmental program at any particular institution is specifically designed to assist students in developing the competencies needed for success in that particular school's regular freshman and core curriculum classes. Thus, attempts to transfer competencies developed at a two-year institution to course work at a senior institution will not always succeed.

EXEMPLARS AND PROBLEMS IN THE DELIVERY OF DEVELOPMENTAL SERVICES

Of the many developmental programs across the nation, several can be identified as exemplars in terms of their success. This section describes selected programs, delineates specific factors of success, and identifies issues and problems inherent to the administration of developmental services.

Although the success of a variety of types of developmental programs can be attributed to any of a number of factors, the two exemplars described here were selected for discussion because they encompass an array of services with an intense focus on the "whole student." The nature of these programs is in keeping with the elements of the most pervasive definitions of developmental programs (see earlier section).

One program addresses the "whole student" in terms of a curriculum that is sensitive to the ethnic background the individual student brings to the educational environment. The other program addresses the "whole student" in terms of personal, interpersonal, affective, and cognitive domains. Both programs incorporate a multidimensional, interdisciplinary approach designed to improve the success ratios of high-risk students of minority or nontraditional groups that are typical of the demographic profile presented in section 2.

The huge and inconsistent literature on developmental programs is best reflected in the subsection below on "Problems." (See also section 5 for additional information on program results.)

From a global perspective, successful programs are found to have two characteristics in common: comprehensiveness in their support services and institutionalization within the academic mainstream.

Profiles of Two Successful Programs

The first exemplar, the University of Minnesota's General College Retention Program, is described as an academic support service designed to assist, encourage, and retain high-risk students (Zanoni 1982). The program consists of three individualized packages geared to meet the academic and support service needs of three particular ethnic or racial minority groups (Native American, Chicano/Latino, and African-American students). Students are recruited by the University of Minnesota Office of Minority and Special Student Affairs (OMSSA), and they attend an OMSSA Summer Institute prior to their first fall quarter. Services are delivered to students within the following model of integrated educational modules:

- skills development courses (language modules),
- subject matter modules,

- support services, and
- individualized course assistance.

The skills development courses are based on language modules designed to improve the students' reading, writing, and speaking skills. The language modules were created in recognition of program participants' general weaknesses in fundamental skills. The subject matter modules focus on the cultural values of each ethnic and/or racial group. Examples of courses in the subject matter module are Issues in Native American Education, Contemporary Chicano Issues, and Afro-American Literature. These courses are taught by "ethnic" instructors, who seek to enhance the students' sense of cultural identity and pride. Support services include tutorial assistance, availability of survival information, career planning assistance, and counseling and advising. The program description indicates the use of ethnic tutors, advisors, and counselors whenever possible. Individualized course assistance is provided for program participants who are enrolled in the General College subject matter courses, such as mathematics and science. The courses are taught by regular faculty, but special tutorial and support mechanisms are arranged for the particularly needy special students.

The program reports that its overall retention rate increased in its second year, from 59 percent in 1979–80 to 70 percent in 1980–81. The general improvement in retention rate for students within the developmental program has been attributed to several reasons. The program report cites the selectivity of its recruitment efforts; the refining of course offerings to include only those courses, methods, and support services that have proved effective in meeting the needs of its students; the commitment of instructors to the objectives of the program and their levels of competence and sense of cooperation; and students' identification with the objectives of the program as a result of the cohesive inclusion of ethnic or racial minority instructors as team members.

The level of effectiveness of the Minnesota program is also reflected in "the nature, scope and content of the evaluation [plan] . . . evidence that the program's measurement instruments are adequate to assess the impact of the total program on student retention" (Zanoni 1982, p. 7).

The second exemplar, the Freshman Studies Program (FSP) at Livingstone College/Rutgers University, is a developmental program for nontraditional students that aims to improve the retention and academic achievement of the target population (Marshall 1981). Although conclusive evidence is not available, preliminary findings (Marshall 1981) indicate that students who participated in the program performed better than their counterparts from the year before the program was initiated. The program's statement of purpose acknowledges the idea that "the most crucial factor in freshman attrition seems to be the degree of congruence of 'fit' between the student and the college environment . . . academically, socially and motivationally" (p. 1). Thus, the Rutgers program was designed to attend to the total learning experience of the students by focusing on cognitive, personal, and interpersonal domains.

An additional focus of the program is creating "an atmosphere which will promote student satisfaction and achievement" by way of providing a "success oriented and accepting environment" (p. 5). The program facilitators indicated a commitment to maintaining the success-oriented environment by viewing their participants as "being as capable of success" as regularly admitted students.

The target population for the FSP includes every student enrolled through the Equal Opportunity Fund. A New Jersey Basic Skills Test is used as the basis for assigning students to either of two groups. Level I students are designated to participate in basic skills classes in reading, writing, and mathematics, and in content courses selected by staff to match the student's basic skill level. Level I students are also assigned to a weekly counseling group and sessions of a College Survival seminar. All other students are assigned only to the counseling group, the College Survival seminar, and one content course. The selection of content courses includes such titles as African-American Experience in America and Puerto Rican Studies.

Other features of the FSP that are said to have contributed to its success are the implementation of the interdisciplinary team teaching concept; a reading course entitled Analytical and Critical Reading; a support unit of faculty from the various disciplines who volunteer to work with the program and who are interested in innovative teaching methods and underprepared students and are willing to include FSP students in their regular courses; peer counselors to facilitate outreach efforts and freshman adjustment by co-leading counseling group sessions; block scheduling matched to a content area course; and the percentage of class time spent applying the skills taught in reading, writing, and mathematics to the assignments in a specific content course. The program also seeks to enhance student development by means of parental orientation and involvement, continuous monitoring, and providing evaluative feedback to the students.

The potential for effectiveness in the Rutgers program also rests, in part, in its evaluation plan. The initial two-pronged design, for example, consisted of a comparative study of freshmen groups in two consecutive years, the control (nonparticipant) preprogram group and the treatment (participant) group in the first year of the program, as well as evaluations from all individuals involved in the project (students, administrators, faculty, and staff) (Marshall 1981).

It is evident that personnel and program design are critical determinants. The influential factors underlying each of these variables are discussed below.

Factors of Success: Personnel

Particular personnel competencies are identified in the literature as critical elements in the success of developmental programs. Good developmental teachers are described as those who set attainable goals, encourage students, provide continuous positive feedback as reinforcement, and make students aware of their strengths and their own ability to control their successes and failures (Ross and Roe 1986). From a collection of 113 professional competencies of remedial instructors, the following eight categories were established:

1. manifest personal qualities
2. application of interpersonal skills
3. ability to structure and sequence skill competencies
4. instructional planning skills
5. instructional delivery
6. assessment of student progress
7. public relations and,
8. program administration (Dickens 1980).

Practitioners warn against the involuntary placement of faculty in developmental positions, because such faculty are likely to resent the assignment and manifest negative attitudes that will transmit to students, who often bring their own negative attitudes to such programs. The combination of negative teacher attitudes and negative student attitudes can be counterproductive. It is also suggested that faculty in developmental courses maintain contact with regular academic faculty on their campus; if possible, teach regular courses in their disciplines; and contribute to the sharing of information about their students when students are concurrently enrolled in regular and developmental courses.

The counselor also plays a vital role in the success of developmental programs. Students enrolled in remedial courses often have poor self-concepts, perceive the campus as an alienating environment, have poor self-management skills, have test anxiety, or have a combination of these problems, which counselors are trained to address in a way that can assist students in positive self-direction. It is suggested that counseling be available to all developmental students from the preregistration/orientation phase until the end of their stay in the institution.

Finally, tutors are highly instrumental in the success of developmental programs. In order to succeed in the course requirements, many developmental students need additional assistance beyond the basic classroom instruction. Tutorial instruction may be provided by regular instructors, developmental instructors, or trained peer tutors. Tutors must be skilled in keeping the student on task, providing positive reinforcement, setting appropriate goals, keeping instruction focused, and monitoring the student's progress (Ross and Roe 1986).

Factors of Success: Program Design

The literature analyzes elements common to successful programs from a variety of perspectives ranging from the very broad to the specific. From a global perspective, successful programs are found to have two characteristics in common: comprehensiveness in their support services and institutionalization within the academic mainstream. A variety of factors that influence the effective structuring of learning improvement have been grouped into the following five basic categories: (1) decisions relating to goals and rationale, (2) instructional methods, (3) institutional policies and standards, (4) professional and paraprofessional staff and roles, and (5) the evaluation of learning improvement programs (Keimig 1983).

Each of the basic categories of implementation identified above has been targeted in the literature as involving specific operational functions that are considered essential for the success of a program. For decisions relating to goals and rationale, specific program needs are a comprehensive, structured developmental program that includes mathematics, English, reading, study skills, and support services, such as tutoring and counseling (Ross and Roe 1986), and an interface of basic skills courses and regular, subsequent courses (J. Roueche, Baker, and S. Roueche 1984).

The program needs most commonly attributed to success in the area of instructional methods are flexible programs designed to meet the needs of different students (Ross and Roe 1986) and multiple learning systems (J. Roueche, Baker, and S. Roueche 1984) for use with the individual. Specific institutional policies and standards most frequently identified for program success are required entry-level tests and mandated basic skills courses for students who lack minimum competencies; a limited number of courses allowed for remediating deficiencies; adequate funding (Ross and Roe 1986); and strong administrative support and awarding of credit (J. Roueche, Baker, and S. Roueche 1984).

Vital program needs regarding professional and paraprofessional staff and their roles are commonly defined as a full-time director to supervise and coordinate the program and staff, faculty who are committed to the program and provided with ongoing training (Ross and Roe 1986), and peer tutors (J. Roueche, Baker, and S. Roueche 1984). Finally, the continuous evaluation of all aspects of the program, particularly the success rate of students after they leave the program (Ross and Roe 1986) and the effectiveness with which basic skills courses interface with regular, subsequent courses (J. Roueche, Baker, and S. Roueche 1984) are considered vital to the ongoing success of developmental programs.

General Criticisms

In the same national study from which J. Roueche, Baker, and S. Roueche (1984) documented success factors commonly associated with developmental programs, it was also found that in a majority of these programs some basic faults are recurrent. Although students are required to do more reading, writing, and figuring in basic skills courses than in regular courses, half the students in many developmental classes do not purchase textbooks, basic skills courses are only loosely related to other courses in the college, exams in developmental courses are typically objective (short answers, true-false, or multiple choice), and the evaluation of developmental courses is entirely inadequate (Budig 1986). In a close look at one institution, Budig also found that students had very little opportunity to enhance and practice the basic skills taught within the courses offered.

Another common criticism of developmental programs is that they are not cost effective (Ross and Roe 1986). These programs are expensive because they require special materials, equipment, and space; the pupil/teacher ratio must be limited; and many tutorial hours must be provided in addition to classroom instruction. In 1981, for example, the state of Georgia spent more than $6 million on developmental programs, and Ohio State University spent between $10 million and $12 million in the same year ("Toughening Up" 1982). This criticism may not be well founded, however, because the impact of any educational experience may actually be very difficult to measure accurately or appropriately for all of its participants when any one given exposure may generate different levels of fulfillment, achievement, or meaning for different individuals within a group. Degree completion, persistence, grade point average, other traditional measures of institutional effectiveness, and retention studies do not necessarily tap the cost-effect value of developmental instruction for many participants.

Problems
This subsection discusses problems and issues that often attend implementation of developmental programs. Many of these problems are contingent on each other such that one tends to exacerbate the other and, thereby, thwarts the effective delivery of services to possibly larger numbers of students. Any of these problems or a combination of them can also be identified in programs that are considered successful.

Funding
Although legislation now entitles all American youths to financial assistance for postsecondary education if they fall within the designated limit on household income, the unreliable funding of some developmental programs leads to a path of tenuous existence. In many instances, impressive sums of money are designated for developmental programs at the

system-wide level, but the allocation of such funds to the various schools within the system does not necessarily coincide with the particular needs of each institution. Where funds are said to be distributed equally, some recipient institutions must make more intensive use of faculty, staff, equipment, and facilities in order to meet the special demands of its disadvantaged students. The most common problem related to funding has been threats of cancellation of grant funding (Mallery, Bullock, and Madden 1987).

Recruitment of Staff

Recruitment of program staff remains a constant problem for most institutions due to staff turnover (H. Astin et al. 1972). Political infighting at some schools has also intensified the problem. These problems are attributed to insecurity, the temporary nature of funding in many instances, and the low stature of staff as perceived by chairpersons of other departments (Sharma 1977). Instructors for many programs are hired as non-tenure track and/or temporary faculty and, thus, job insecurity is heightened, competent individuals are reluctant to pursue such positions, and incentives for scholarly contributions in curriculum development, research, or service are scarce. Poor staff morale and faculty burnout also exacerbate the problem of recruitment and retention of individuals who are needed for the successful delivery of developmental services. Salaries that are not competitive, cutbacks in travel reimbursement, few opportunities for upward mobility within universities, and a shift toward more stringent tenure and promotional requirements have also created obstacles to the successful operation of developmental programs (Mallery, Bullock, and Madden 1987).

Minimum Admission Standards and Placement Standards

Standards vary within systems at various institutional levels such that there is no consistent indicator of what is held to be the threshold of preparedness or underpreparedness (Abraham 1986). Within an institutional level (university, four-year college, two-year college), minimum admission criteria now vary across categories of entering freshmen (e.g., for athletes, the minimum total SAT score of 700 is set by proposition 48 of the National Collegiate Athletic Association, while other entering freshmen may qualify with total scores of less than

'00). Students are also accepted with minimal entrance scores and then deemed by faculty as too deficient to be taught effectively. Where systems allow each institution to determine its own admission standards by a combination of high school grade point average and SAT or American College Test scores that is said to predict success or failure, there is cause to consider whether the process is adequate—whether all who are accepted or rejected are accurately predicted for success or for failure.

In a survey of remedial/developmental programs in 489 public two-year and four-year colleges in the Southern Regional Educational Board states, Abraham (1986) found the following:

> Colleges and universities use few common standards to make placement decisions . . . In the SREB states, almost 100 combinations of about 70 different tests in the areas of reading, writing, and mathematics are used to place students in either college degree-credit or remedial/development courses . . . It is also reasonable to assume that the large variety of tests in use implies a lack of uniform standards for what is usually considered "college-level" work (pp. 1–4).

At least 10 instruments were identified (across the aggregate of responding institutions) for each subject area placement process (see table 2).

Affirmative Action

Although many developmental programs were instituted as a part of the movement toward desegregation, there is often a pervasive misconception that affirmative action is the sole purpose of such programs. At most institutions at which desegregation has ever been an issue, the minority students within the developmental program are a small percentage of the program's enrollment. Another misconception is that the developmental program exists solely for the purpose of serving those who are underprepared as a result of disadvantages. At many institutions, the student population of developmental programs includes individuals from affluent and middle-class homes. In some instances, foreign students speaking English as a second language have been enrolled in developmental programs because there were no other services to assist them in overcoming language barriers. Despite such an enrollment

Many developmental programs continue to suffer the stigma of being perceived primarily as a vehicle for affirmative action—particularly for desegregation.

TABLE 2

COLLEGE PLACEMENT TESTS USED BY SREB SURVEY RESPONDENTS, BY RANK, FOR READING, WRITING, AND MATHEMATICS 1985-86

Rank	READING Placement Test		WRITING Placement Test		MATHEMATICS Placement Test	
1	Nelson—Denny	121*	ACT-English	72*	In-house/institutionally developed	118*
2	ACT—Combined	43*	In-house/institutionally developed	66	ACT—Mathematics	71
3	MAPS—Descriptive Test of Language Skills	37	Writing Sample/Essay	57	SAT—Mathematics	47
4	SAT—Verbal	35	Test of Standard Written English	53	MAPS—Descriptive Test of Mathematics Skills Elementary Algebra	36
5	ASSET	29	ACT—Combined	36	State/System Developed Test	29
6	State/System Developed Test	27	SAT—Verbal	28	MAPS—Descriptive Test of Mathematic Skills—Intermediate Algebra	27
7	ACT—Social Studies	26	State/System Developed Test	28	ACT—Combined	
8	MAPS—Comparative Guidance Placement Test—Reading	23	ASSET—Language Usage	24	MAPS—Comparative Guidance Placement—Mathematics C Test	23
9	ACT—English	18	MAPS—Comparative Guidance Placement Test—Writing	24	MAPS—Descriptive Test of Mathematics Skills—Arithmetic	22
10	Test of Adult Basic Education	12	Assessment and Placement Services of Community Colleges—Essay	15	ASSET—Numerical	17

Source: Abraham (1986). Reproduced with permission of Southern Regional Education Board.

mix, many developmental programs continue to suffer the stigma of being perceived primarily as a vehicle for affirmative action—particularly for desegregation. This misconception was born of an age of accountability in which, to a considerable extent, desegregation orders have periodically driven developmental program policies and procedures (Mallery, Bullock, and Madden 1987) as well as institutional policies systemwide.

Retention

Many retention studies indicate that substantial numbers of students who exit developmental programs do successfully complete degree programs. Many other studies indicate that students emerging from such programs do as well as or often better than other near-marginal students who were regularly admitted, particularly in certain core courses. Unfortunately, there are also many reports of significant numbers of students who are unsuccessful in completing developmental programs or in completing degree programs after exiting them.

Caution should be exercised in considering the overall outcome of retention for developmental students because many institutions have only recently begun to conduct and report retention studies and cannot provide pertinent information with regard to completion of four-year degree programs. (A five-year period is generally considered in order to report retention rates for completion of the four-year degree program.) Currently, many systems are only able to provide information on retention rates and degree completion for their junior or community colleges.

Retention rates also fail to account for many students who may, at some point, "stop out" of school and/or transfer to another system and go on to complete degree programs over an extended period of time. At their worst, retention rates emphasize numbers of individual who remain enrolled and numbers of individuals who complete degree programs, while benefits accrued to individuals receiving developmental instruction and participating in campus life, regardless of short-term academic achievements, have been sorely overlooked with regard to long-term effects on consumerism, voting behavior, self-awareness, and the quality of life in general. Withdrawal from college during or after a developmental program does not necessarily predict continued failure, although, ideally, all students who are allowed to enter such a program should be able to meet completion requirements at some point in time if permitted to pursue completion for as long as they demonstrate effort and progress.

The retention of students during their enrollment in a developmental program is also said to be closely associated with whether the program is fully integrated into the mainstream of the institution or set apart. Where programs are set apart, the programs and students often suffer (Davis, Burkheimer, and Borders-Patterson 1975).

Discriminatory Testing

In view of the affirmative action stigma placed on developmental programs, it is ironic that, in many instances, the entrance exams used by institutions of higher education for purposes of admissions and placement have been alleged to discriminate against minority groups to the effect that not only are minority applicants denied regular admissions and placed in developmental programs, but they are also denied access to developmental programs in significant numbers. In addition, the admissions tests that place minority students into developmental programs and test preparation courses are alleged to be discriminatory due to the poor preparation students are given prior to retaking the mandated admissions test. In many cases, individuals who scored below the minimum requirement level on institutional admissions tests and were allowed to enroll, on a provisional basis, have still failed to achieve the required minimum score after completing a four-year degree program and retaking the admissions test, sometimes repeatedly. Such results are, no doubt, in conflict with the notion of setting levels of standards for admission and instruction such that the majority of students who are permitted to enter can successfully complete the requirements.

Exit Requirements

Exit requirements have often been set, arbitrarily, in terms of time limitations within which students are required to complete a series of courses and/or demonstrate a particular level of proficiency in a given subject area before they can register for regular course offerings within the same subject area. Quite frequently, substantial numbers of students who are admitted into developmental programs make considerable progress from term to term or from one course level to the next, but they are still unable to meet the minimum exit requirements within the predetermined time limitations. This has been particularly true in instances in which students with extremely low achievement scores or specific deficiencies have been enrolled. On the other hand, some developmental programs conduct courses that are considered more rigorous than certain core course offerings, which leads to a situation in which developmental students may have achieved proficiency in a given area comparable to the proficiency levels of students who were marginally accepted under regular admissions criteria, but at the same time, the developmental students are still unable to perform at the proficiency level arbitrarily designated for exit criteria.

Proficiency Objectives

Although exit requirements are frequently found to be stringent with regard to expected proficiency levels as well as time limitations, there is still some question as to whether enough students who do exit developmental programs are adequately prepared to succeed beyond the core course level. Where retention rates indicate that substantial numbers of developmental students do not complete degree programs, it is suspected that the emphasis of course content in the developmental program is based primarily on developing the skills necessary to meet exit requirements—in essence, merely to pass exit tests. Starks (1982) indicates that a successful program should show evidence of helping students to complete regular course work and, thereby, reduce attrition. Thus, a critical consideration for developmental programs is whether enrolled students are trained to develop a capacity for independent inquiry and problem solving.

Holistic vs. Skills Approaches

Within some developmental programs there exist conflicting opinions as to whether instruction should evolve from a holistic or a specific skills focus—whether instruction should be based on the use of whole contexts and global communication and interpretation or the application of specific and isolated skills to materials designed or selected for such specific purposes. In instances in which students with very low ability levels are involved, the exclusive use of holistic approaches presents a problem in that these students' progress remains thwarted by a lack of remediation in a particular skill for which passing the threshold of proficiency is essential to more global and holistic competencies.

As an example, students who lack total proficiency in the specific reading skill of phonetic decoding will be at a loss to decipher certain individual words, let alone draw conclusions, make inferences, and summarize a whole written passage. At another level, there are those students who are adept at drawing conclusions and summarizing information, exclusively on the basis of given facts, but who are unable to make inferences until given specific instruction and practice in the differences and similarities between conclusions and inferences and the logic required in deducing new information from that which is already presented. The overall goal of the Rutgers University FSP developmental program is one of improving the skills deficits of the students that are identified by their profiles (Marshall 1981). It is stated that the Rutgers mission is to help students learn, in a concrete manner, how skills acquired in reading, writing, and mathematics are applied to their regular course work.

Lack of Relativity

This problem is reflected in the curriculum of many developmental programs in terms of both the lack of interrelatedness of content and subject area and the lack of relativity of content to the backgrounds and immediate concerns of students. Because most institutions of higher education conduct developmental programs within the same daily instructional time constraints as other course offerings, an automatic limitation is placed on the amount of remediation that can be expected to occur in a given span of time. Thus, relevance in the teaching/learning process must be optimized in order to increase motivation and interest in tasks for which students may have developed disinterest, may have experienced failure, or may have assessed as useless pursuits bearing little relevance to real-world and immediate survival concerns. In many programs the basic skills are taught under the auspices of separate subject components (English, mathematics, reading) with separate curriculum and separate content area materials. Even in instances in which the focus of one component, such as writing, is stressed in the approach to another component (reading)—the materials used and topics covered are often totally different. Moreover, curriculum and materials are often found to be insensitive to the cultural backgrounds, interests, survival skills, and other real-world demands that are inherent and necessary to various cultural groups within the student population. Lipman (1980) argues to this point as follows:

> *If the education process were to be redesigned . . . the overall*
> *objective of such a design would be an educational system*
> *of maximum intrinsic value (as contrasted with a system*

whose values are purely instrumental and extrinsic), max-
imum meaningfulness and rationality, and maximum
methodological unity and consistency . . . the school must
be defined by the nature of education and not education
by the nature of the school . . . anything that helps us dis-
cover meaning in life is educational, and the schools are
educational only insofar as they do facilitate such discovery
(p. 3).

Lack of Academic Recognition

Lack of academic recognition is a symptom of the stigma suffered by developmental programs in terms of course credit
equivalents and in terms of opposition to the concept of
equity in higher education. At the institutional level, developmental programs are often denied equal academic recognition in that students enrolled in developmental programs
usually receive no college-level credit although they may be
given institutional credit. Thus, faculty and administrators
in other disciplines hesitate to acknowledge any equivalence
in scholarly rank to those faculty in developmental programs
who hold the same title (e.g., assistant professor). At all levels,
from the highest position of governmental influence to the
single average citizen, on the campus or in the community,
there is often a reluctance to accept the notion of equal educational opportunity for all individuals, which results in lack
of academic recognition for developmental programs.

The Imminent Threat of Discontinuance

At the same time that the various institutions are attempting
to serve the diversified learning needs of increasing numbers
of individuals who do not meet regular admissions criteria
but who wish to pursue the benefits of higher education, various factions within the public sector have questioned the
efficacy, relevance, feasibility, and academic status of such
programs within their respective institutions and among the
larger educational community. In the state of Georgia, for
example, where the Governor's Committee on Postsecondary
Education has recommended the discontinuance of developmental studies programs as soon as new secondary and
postsecondary graduation and admissions criteria are met,
there is controversy. It is evident that although the high school
graduating class of 1988 was the first to face the new admission and placement criteria of the Southern Association of

Colleges and Schools, the impact of this new trend on the need for developmental programs will be very gradual.

From a discussion of the implications of the new criteria for developmental studies programs in the University System of Georgia (Ervin and Tomlinson 1986), the critical factors that will ultimately affect developmental programs are teacher training, legislation for need-based funding, and the nature of assessment and evaluation processes at both the secondary and postsecondary levels. These factors will determine if, when, or how the purpose, content, or scope of the developmental programs will change. A considerable amount of time will elapse before significant numbers of teachers and students will be able to actualize the new criteria. Undoubtedly, there will still be the same, if not greater, numbers of minority and educationally disadvantaged students who will not meet the new criteria at the outset.

PROGRAM EVALUATION

Different methods are used for program evaluation at various institutions. The type of evaluation process that a particular institution may choose is most likely determined by the overall profile of the institution. A number of components that differentiate among programs have been identified (Bers 1987): program objectives, credit and grades, modes of instruction, timing and duration of remedial education activities in a student's college studies, and the status and characteristics of remedial faculty and staff. Other critical components are the classification of students, testing and placement, and organization and funding.

Program evaluation provides a monitoring system with which to assess effectiveness and facilitate improvement; it is by no means a panacea in terms of serving to ameliorate all of the many problems that a program may experience. The ultimate purpose of program evaluation should be to determine whether the program enables underprepared students to acquire skills necessary to complete college (Ross and Roe 1986). Types of criteria used for evaluation can be categorized as follows: inputs or efforts (resources), performance (results or outcomes), adequacy of performance, efficiency, and process (Bers 1987).

Evaluation data can be obtained through informal procedures as well as formal procedures. Informal methods may involve student assessments of instructors and counselors and overall program effectiveness; staff can assess the utility of various teaching techniques and materials; and regular faculty can provide feedback on the performance of former developmental students (Ross and Roe 1986). Formal procedures involve carefully designed, systematically administered measures that may require the identification of numerous variables that are monitored, cross-referenced, and stored for long-term and comparative analyses as well as immediate feedback. Formal evaluation may be coordinated by the campus institutional research office or the research component of the developmental program, or the collection and storage of data may be a joint effort.

Assessments of Program Evaluation

Assessments of the validity and reliability of developmental program evaluations over the past three decades prompt some skepticism as to the accuracy of this research in its efforts to determine the effectiveness and value of programs. The re-

Program evaluation provides a monitoring system with which to assess effectiveness and facilitate improvement; it is by no means a panacea in terms of serving to ameliorate all of the many problems that a program may experience.

search design of studies showing positive results from developmental programs prior to the 1960s has been criticized as faulty (Cross 1976).

One pervasive observation of the nature of educational evaluation has been that although evaluation of student performance is frequent in all levels of American education, careful appraisal of educational programs has been rare (Wilkerson 1966).

Lack of emphasis on systematic program evaluation is evident in procedures set forth in the guidelines for programs for the "new" student under the Special Services for Disadvantaged Students (SSDS), funded by the Office of Education, Department of Health, Education and Welfare, in institutions of higher education in the late 1960s and early 1970s. The 36-page application information and program manual for the SSDS contains one paragraph on evaluation and research, which (1) prohibits the use of control groups and (2) calls for the establishment of mechanisms to respond to student evaluation (U.S. Department of Health, Education and Welfare 1970). The manual provides no other guidelines for evaluation. Subsequently, an Office of Education annual evaluation report states that systematic efforts at evaluation of educational programs had a short history and that those programs, individually and collectively, had not yet met the objective of redressing various inequalities (U.S. Department of Health, Education and Welfare 1972).

State-supported programs have produced another body of evaluative data. These programs, accountable to the state legislature that appropriates funds, have usually incorporated a research effort. New York, for example, has provided funds to public and private in-state institutions for financial aid and supportive services to residents who exhibit potential for successful completion of an associate or bachelor's degree (Higher Education Opportunity Program 1970). The evaluation of the progress of participating institutions was based primarily on self-evaluations and on-site visitations. Additional evaluations by an outside agency delineated the following for the state legislature: per student state aid allocations, enrollment, student retention rate, and the relationship of retention to various student characteristics, such as sex, marital status, and occupation of father (Human Affairs Research Center 1970). There was no attempt, however, to consider program characteristics, such as tutoring, counseling, or the remedial curriculum, as functions of student retention rate.

In numerous instances, program effectiveness has been based on varying criteria for measuring improvement, ranging from specific skill performance to grade point average, matriculation, and persistence; applied to a variety of types of schools, selective and public; within the various regions of the nation; and among various ethnic groups. The diversity of variables from program to program confounds systematic comparative assessments. During the rapid establishment of record numbers of developmental programs in the late 1960s and early 1970s, however, individual evaluation reports reflect many positive results as well as some negative or unchanged performance trends among the populations assessed.

Focus and Findings
of Program Evaluations

Positive results have been documented in evaluations of specific services. Some examples follow: reading instruction by student tutors and by faculty tutors against a control group (Yuthas 1971); a pre-community college summer session for African-American students (Gattman 1967); a summer program with a reading and study skills emphasis (Kling 1972); a summer orientation for disadvantaged and minority students at selective colleges (Oskamp, Hodges, Thompson, and Spuck 1970); assistance from graduate student tutors for high-risk students in advanced courses (Menges, Max, and Trumpeter 1972); a reading and writing emphasis with a reduced load at a southern public university (Algier 1972); student-to-student counseling on study habits and instruction in study skills at a southwestern public university (W. Brown 1971); and individual counseling and instruction at an eastern public university (Kaye 1972).

Fewer negative reports are found. Specific services from which negative results or unchanged performance was documented include a summer readiness program at a selective western college (Klingelhofer and Longacre 1972); a dual-function counselor/tutor program for African-American students at a southern university (Wilson 1970); and a reading rate and/or study skills program (with varying emphases) evaluated against a control group (Belcher 1971; DiSalvi 1971).

Comprehensive programs characterized by multidimensional efforts incorporating skills development curriculum, tutorial assistance, and academic and nonacademic counseling have rarely been evaluated systematically. Of those that have been widely documented, however, most report positive results (Brody, Harris, and Lachica 1968; Bucklin and Bucklin 1971; Tetlow 1970; Urban Problem Solving Program 1970; and Wenrich 1971).

During this period, there was a call for the evaluation of specific programming efforts in order to isolate those aspects of developmental education programs that are most effective in curbing attrition and promoting academic success (Gordon 1970; Simmons 1970). The College Discovery and Development Program of the City University of New York is one program that conducted evaluations in accordance with this objective. Where tutorial assistance was provided by college students for program participants, a five-pronged evaluation focused on other similar programs, the tutors, tutees, teachers, and parents (Brody, Harris, and Lachica 1968). Ross and Roe (1986) cite a review of the research (Maxwell 1980) that indicates that many reading improvement programs, particularly the individualized, counseling-oriented, and voluntary programs, did produce improved grades, and they refer to an analysis of 60 evaluative studies of developmental programs (C. Kulik, J. Kulik, and Schwalb 1983) that found programs "generally worthwhile." They also refer, however, to the analysis of two major studies of postsecondary schools (J. Roueche, Baker, and S. Roueche 1984), which concluded that few institutions evaluate their developmental programs adequately.

Evaluation Designs and Implications
The designs of developmental program evaluations have been reviewed substantially in the literature (Budig 1986; Joplin and Brown 1981; Ross and Roe 1986; Wright and Cahalan 1985). A comprehensive model for the design of program evaluation includes preprogram and post-program measures, a grouping statistic, and some form of control group for comparison. These basic guidelines allow for pretest measures in the form of aptitude or achievement test scores. Post-program measures should include short-range measures, such as final grade or final examination scores, and long-range measures, such as the student's grade in the next course, grade point average after a specified number of semesters, credits earned, or persistence in college (Akst and Hecht 1980).

The evaluation design that is considered to be the most straightforward—the single-group pretest/post-program comparison has been criticized for a serious limitation (Budig 1986), that is, the design addresses only the remedial population and uses two equivalent forms of the same test for preprogram and post-program measures. Budig recommends that this procedure be used only if there is no other alternative and only if all evaluative biases are controlled for. Because withholding remedial opportunities from those who need it (for purposes of obtaining a control group) would be considered unethical, a recommended strategy for bypassing this problem is to take as the control group students whose preprogram measures indicate the need for remedial work but who evade it (Budig 1986).

Four evaluative designs that have been recommended (Akst and Hecht 1980) are outlined below:

1. The remediated-exempted comparison, in which the performance of the exempted population is used as the standard for assessing the achievement of remediated students.
2. The norm-group comparison, in which the standard is the performance of a national population.
3. The cross-group comparison, which compares the effectiveness of two different remedial programs, usually at separate institutions.
4. The historical comparison, which contrasts the effectiveness of a current program with that of one previously offered at the same school.

Another popular source of program evaluation information is the national sample survey, which provides data on how developmental programs are operating collectively. In one such survey, respondents evaluated the success or effectiveness of such program aspects as courses, support services, organization and policy, and outcome for remedial students (Wright and Cahalan 1985). A scale of 1 (low) to 5 (high) was used. Wright and Cahalan found that most respondents rated their programs moderately high, overall, with a mean score of 3.8 for many items. What is particularly interesting is that the highest ratings were given to teacher attitude, teacher training, and curriculum content and structure, and the lowest ratings were given to program evaluation, degree completion rate, and breadth of course offerings. Wright and Calahan report that 30 percent of the survey respondents gave program evaluation a below-average rating.

A particular weakness found in evaluation processes, as indicated by the same survey, is the lack of focus on retention information. Wright and Cahalan found that 63 percent of colleges reported that they kept records on the percentage of total freshmen retained but only 35 percent reported that they kept separate records on the percentage of remedial students retained. The survey also indicated that retention records were more frequently kept by four-year than two-year schools. (Two-year schools have a larger percentage of part-time students, who are difficult to track and whose behavioral patterns are difficult to interpret.)

Finally, national survey approaches have also been used to conduct collective program evaluations on the basis of special interest foci, such as race. In a comparative study of

TABLE 3
EVALUATION CATEGORIES USED FOR THE COMPARISION OF PROGRAMS

Institutional Characteristics

type of institution	institutional setting
calendar year	existence of developmental reading
admissions policy	course status
length of operation	program description
student placement	

Enrollment and Retention

institutional enrollment	classification of students served
enrollment in program	completion rate
student matriculation	

Faculty Status

faculty rank and tenure	staff supervision
staff composition	tenure of administrator
instructor evaluation	

Program Design

| success of program | project evaluation |
| departmental affiliation | method of conducting reading courses |

Instructional Delivery

| instructional practices | instructor/student ratio |
| support services | |

Course Credit

| credit hours earned | type of credit |
| student evaluation | |

Funding

| source of funding | percentage of funding |

developmental reading programs in traditionally African-American colleges and universities and their white counterparts (Joplin and Brown 1981), the variables of reading instruction and racial composition of 113 institutions were the primary factors under consideration. The major areas of analysis were institutional characteristics, enrollment and retention, faculty status, program design, instructional delivery, course credit, and funding. Several institutional characteristics, enrollment and retention characteristics, and additional areas of analysis were targeted (see table 3).

A four-stage model for evaluating developmental programs allows for the use of all of the above-mentioned criteria as they apply to a particular program and its subjectivity to constant change. In stage one, activities within the developmental program are evaluated (for a sample of how this data might be collected, see table 4 on the next page). In stage two, the match between the developmental program and the mainstream curriculum is evaluated. In stage three, student progress and faculty, staff, and administrative judgments are used to reassess the goals of both the developmental program and the mainstream courses. For example, if there is a significant difference between the percentage reported for grades achieved by regular and developmental students in mainstream courses, then the point of difference (subject area) would indicate that aspect of the developmental program that would deserve closer attention for reevaluation of activities in stage one. Finally, in stage four, the measures previously used for evaluation are reconsidered in terms of their appropriateness for new program goals (Clowes 1984b).

Despite the available expertise on program evaluation design for developmental education, the literature also reflects the fact that honest efforts to conduct meaningful evaluations are still hampered by traditional obstacles that are pervasive in the educational setting. The difficulties in collecting data, controlling variables, allocating time for such purposes, and securing institutional support, among others, are some of the traditional pitfalls to which the evaluation of developmental programs is subject (Dempsey 1986).

TABLE 4

MODEL FOR EVALUATING DEVELOPMENTAL PROGRAMS

Stage One: Performance of Students in Developmental Studies Courses

Quarter	Grade Distribution A B C D F I	Mean Grade	Number Enrolled	Number Exit	Percent Exit
Summer					
English					
Mathematics					
Reading					
Fall					
English					
Mathematics					
Reading					
Winter					
English					
Mathematics					
Reading					
Spring					
English					
Mathematics					
Reading					

Stage Two: A Comparison of Performance in Selected Core Curriculum Courses: Developmental Studies Students and Regularly Enrolled Students

Selected Core Curriculum Courses	Total Enrollment		Grade of D or Better		Grade of C or Better	
	Regularly Enrolled Students N	Developmental Studies Students N	Regularly Enrolled Students %	Developmental Studies Students %	Regularly Enrolled Students %	Developmental Studies Students %
Eng 101						
Eng 102						
Math 100						
Sos 105						
Psy 101						
Pol 101						
His 251						
His 252						
Spc 108						
Ele 102						

CHANGES IN EDUCATION AND THE
CHALLENGE TO DEVELOPMENTAL CURRICULUM

Throughout this century, instructional theories on what should be taught, how it should be taught, and the extent to which instruction can be mastered by various individuals or populations have been based largely on concepts of the measurement of intelligence. A standardized procedure for the measurement of intelligence, the Stanford-Binet Intelligence Quotient, still in use, was initially developed in the early 1900s. Since then, psychometricians and other psychological theorists have explored the measurement of intelligence, refuted the concept of measuring intelligence by claiming that mental processes could not be observed or measured accurately, suggested that intelligence is hereditary, and more recently, turned to the inclusion of environment, experience, and the use of information processes as factors in the measurement of intelligence (Sternberg 1977).

Mainly through decades of low expectations for masses of citizens, we have perpetuated unnecessary academic failure through self-fulfilling prophecy.

During the 1980s many changes in educational programs have been planned. There have been new commitments to excellence, new criteria for accreditation, and new philosophies of instructional practice. Although new courses have been charted, there is still skepticism about goals and intentions with regard to compensatory education. Some of the most promising directions for curriculum have been delineated in Sternberg's (1984) program for training intelligence, Feuerstein's (1980) program of instrumental enrichment, and Lipman's (1980) program of philosophy in the classroom. Lipman has made valuable criticisms of remedial programs, and he warns that much restructuring will be necessary:

Over and over again, we have recourse to remediation rather than to redesign . . . the fundamental source of the system's failure to distribute education effectively . . . remains unexamined, and the increasingly vast sums are poured into efforts to compensate for the inefficiency of the compensatory efforts . . . We [should be] assuming that the only way to make compensatory education work is not to approach it as a . . . compensatory device, but to design it so as to promise educational excellence for all young people (pp. 3–5).

As a preface to Cross's (1981) discussion of adults as learners, the Commission on Non-traditional Study made the following statement:

Most of us agreed that non-traditional study is more an attitude than a system and thus can never be defined except tangentially. This attitude puts the student first and the institution second, concentrates more on the former's need than the latter's convenience, encourages diversity of individual rather than uniform prescription, and deemphasizes time, space, and even course requirements in favor of competence and, where applicable, performance. It has concern for the learner of any age and circumstance, for the degree aspirant as well as the person who finds sufficient reward in enriching life through constant, periodic, or occasional study (p. xv).

Again, as in Lipman's statement, it would seem that there is no effective strategy for compensatory or nontraditional education that would not be an effective strategy or consideration for all education.

Ideally, we should be able to speak of education, rather than education, compensatory education, and nontraditional education. Where nontraditional education will more easily take its place within the concept of what an education ought to be, there will still be the need for a greater effort to resolve the place of compensatory/remedial programs in the realm of education. Mainly through decades of low expectations for masses of citizens, we have perpetuated unnecessary academic failure through self-fulfilling prophecy. Consequently, compensatory programs of the remedial nature will still be necessary for large numbers of individuals for quite some time to come.

To date, psychometric, Piagetian, and cognitive models have been primarily influential in the implementation of instructional programs. As a result of the adoption of psychometric models, students' intelligence, capabilities, and deficits have been measured, analyzed, and approached on the basis of scores in response to performance of a series of tasks, for which subscores have often been averaged. This approach has often obscured the precise characteristics of an individual's strengths and weaknesses. In keeping with Piagetian models, students have often been taught or instructed on the basis of sequences of information, concepts, or tasks in accordance with a predetermined hierarchy of cognitive and psychomotor development. Cognition has received much attention in the past in terms of Piaget's stages of development and, more recently, through the concept of meta-cognition—an individual's understanding of an ability to monitor his own actions (A. Brown 1978; Flavell 1976).

In the 1980s, educational theorists and practitioners have come to recognize the need for intervention programs to train students in the development of intellectual skills (Sternberg 1983). This need is justified by the fact that there has been a marked decline in the intellectual skills of our youth, most visibly demonstrated by SAT test scores. According to Sternberg, however, "college professors don't need SAT scores . . . they can see it in the poorer class performance, and particularly in the poorer reading and writing of their students" (p. 18). Many significant works have been written on methodology for classroom instruction in the basic skills areas, most notably works such as Huey's (1969) *The Psychology and Pedagogy of Reading,* first published in the early 1900s, Pauk's (1962) *How to Study in College,* Bloom's (1956) taxonomy of the levels of questioning for classroom instruction, and Whimbey and Lockhead's (1983) *Analytical Reading and Reasoning,* now in its fourth edition. These approaches to instructional methodology, however, predate the more recently developed theories of training that address the component processes that make up intelligence (Sternberg 1977).

Emerging philosophies of education involve theories that address the student's intelligence, skill development, problem solving, and critical thought from new perspectives of cognitive processes. Sternberg, Feuerstein, and Lipman have been the major proponents of these new perspectives of cognitive processes and cognitive development in terms of broad training programs. Each of these theorists acknowledges the applicability of previous models but also criticizes their limitations as they pertain to prediction, diagnosis, and instruction. Psychometric models have been most severely criticized.

These three recent pioneers in the development of programs for training intelligence have made significant contributions based on the premises that (1) intelligence can be taught, (2) the majority of school children are not being exposed to process training, and (3) standard curricula should be supplemented with training in intellectual skills (Sternberg 1983). Their work has been selected for further discussion here because of the types of populations they have used for the development of their programs and because of the reported success of their programs. Sternberg, a noted Yale scholar and authority on intelligence, has designed a training program that is based on a theory that has been subjected to extensive empirical testing; covers a wide range of intellectual skills, both practical and academic, synthetic as well as analytic; and is relevant to secondary and college-level instruction. In a thorough review of Feuerstein and Lipman's programs, Sternberg (1983) has presented comparative analyses of the strengths and weaknesses of their applications.

Feuerstein's training program is assessed as appropriate for children in the upper grades of elementary school to early high school; for a wide range of ability levels, from retarded to above average; and for a wide range of socioeconomic groups. Moreover, the program appears to be effective in raising intrinsic motivation, self-esteem, and scores on ability tests (Sternberg 1983).

Lipman's program attends to many of the same skills as Feuerstein's program, but by means of a very different approach. The program is assessed as most appropriate for upper elementary schoolchildren, and the content of the materials is found to be highly motivational, effective in raising the level of the student's thinking skills, and applicable to the content areas such that durability and transfer of learning are facilitated (Sternberg 1983).

Sternberg notes that the limitations of his program are its lack of material on deductive thinking or traditional logic and its lesser focus on the contextual aspect of intelligence. He finds the limitations of Feuerstein's program to be in its breadth of skills and low potential for generalizability; Lipman's program limitations are said to be that students with low to average intellectual capacity might not be able to manage the reading and reasoning levels and that lower-class students may not relate to the characters in the program's stories. What is most important, however, is that, given the positive merits of each program, the variance in applicable age ranges, ability levels, or background provides for adaptability to the new diversity in freshman populations of college-level developmental programs.

Although the theoretical perspectives are applicable to teaching/learning at all levels in all educational settings, they should be particularly useful to developmental studies programs if such programs seek to adopt the most exemplary approaches to instruction that are available.

Sternberg: Training Intelligence

Sternberg (1984) examines psychometric models in relation to prediction, diagnosis, and training. He recognizes the utility of psychometrics for predicting future success in a particular educational program or work setting. He views the psychometric model as derived from a set of underlying sources of individual differences, called factors, such as verbal comprehension, verbal fluency, number, spatial visualization, reasoning, memory, and perceptual speed. He considers factor analysis useful for diagnosing individual strengths and weaknesses, but not as useful for prediction, because the factors only suggest broad abilities in which training is necessary.

As for training in intelligence performance, Sternberg indicates that the factors are of minimal usefulness. He explains that, for example, factors do not indicate in what specific aspects of verbal comprehension a student needs training if a verbal comprehension score is too low. He also cautions that when information is obtained about specific factors on a single test, training based on such factors may not be generalizable to other tests or tasks. Essentially, Sternberg refutes the utility of the psychometric model in generating successful training programs because its strengths are not necessarily conducive to such purposes. His criticism of the psychometric model is based on a belief that a theory for training must specify the following:

- competent processes used in performance of tasks which it applies,
- strategies into which these component processes combine,
- internal representations on which these component strategies act,
- executive processes that control the selection of component processes of performance, and
- how these elements combine to interact with different global patterns of ability to produce various levels of successful performance.

Psychometric models usually do not specify these elements.

A most important aspect of Sternberg's theory is his conceptualization of the nature of intelligence in terms of its basic construct, which he explains as follows:

The basic construct is the component. A component is an elementary information process that operates upon internal representations of objects or symbols. Components can be classified on the basis of their functions into five different kinds: metacomponents, performance components, acquisition components, retention components, and transfer components. . . . There can be no doubt that the major variable in the development of the intellect is the metacomponential one. All feedback is filtered through these elements, and if they do not perform their function well, then it won't matter very much what the other kinds of components can do (p. 28).

Intelligence, as explained by Sternberg, is based on the operation of the five components, all interacting primarily through the metacomponential functions to provide the basis for intellectual development throughout the life span. Meta-cognition—understanding how a process works and being able to monitor the process—is widely identified as the basis for effective learning, which is undeveloped in the unsuccessful student. The teaching of study strategies is frequently guided by this concept.

Feuerstein: Instrumental Enrichment

Feuerstein (1980) has also criticized the use of psychometric models in terms of prediction, diagnosis, and instruction. His critique is based on four points: the structure of tests, the exam situation, the orientation of tests, and the interpretation of results. According to Feuerstein, tests usually are not constructed as if to be used in a teaching process that would facilitate the evaluation of the effect of teaching on the capacity of the student in new situations. He describes the exam situation as one in which the interaction is forced, unnatural, nonconducive to learning or performance, and one in which the examiner usually does not act in ways that would develop latent potential in the examinee. The orientation of tests is described as one that emphasizes the products of performance rather than the processes that give rise to the products. Feuerstein also indicates that the psychometric model induces damaging motivational states in individuals (even more so in retarded individuals), which leads to a depression of test performance. Finally, he concludes that the interpretation of test results places an emphasis on aggregates of performance data, when in fact peak scores should be used as an indication of the cognitive potential of the examinee, rather than viewed as error of measurement.

In comparing his own training program to Feuerstein's, Sternberg (1984) indicates that Feuerstein's (1980) program of instrumental enrichment stems from a theory that

- implies a broader base for training, including training of more effective and motivational elements;
- seems to assume some particular deficient functions that characterize the cognitive structure of the deprived individual;
- emphasizes process more than content;
- emphasizes tasks rather than components of the tasks;
- seeks to train potentially deficient cognitive operations indirectly; and
- emphasizes fluid and visual abilities (spatial, form perception, etc.).

Psychometric models have done little to approach instruction in these specific ways.

According to Sternberg, Feuerstein's conceptualization of the nature of intelligence stems from a theory that has three basic parts:

A list of potentially deficient cognitive functions organized around phases of input, elaboration, and output; a cognitive map that can be used to analyze tasks in terms of seven dimensions of analysis; and a theory of development that stresses the role of mediated learning experience in the development of intelligence (p. 22).

Feuerstein's theory of the development of intelligence is said to be based primarily on the concept of mediated learning experience, wherein the development of cognitive structure in an organism can be viewed as a product of two modalities of interaction between the organism and its environment: direct exposure to stimuli and mediated learning. (The former is a much needed intervention for the experientially deficient student, and the latter is inherent to the context of developmental instruction.)

Lipman: Philosophy in the Classroom
Although Lipman (1980) does not address the use of psychometric models of prediction, diagnosis, and instruction

directly, his opposition to psychometric approaches is evident in his discussion of reading:

Reading is . . . the focus of much attention . . . Critics accuse the schools of not teaching reading well, and many schools respond by paying greater . . . attention to reading . . . at the expense of other educational objectives . . . increasingly the stress is on reading, while the thinking processes it was supposed to build are neglected . . . It may seem strange that we urge the teaching of reasoning to improve children's reading, and that . . . reading be seen in turn as a means to help children think, rather than as an end in itself . . . instruction in the procedures of reasoning can be helpful in developing . . . thinking (p. 19).

It is also apparent that Lipman does not adhere to the notion of developmental stages, which are characteristic of Piagetian models. He explains his training approach as follows:

Unlike "atomistic teaching" which introduces a segment of knowledge, drills for it until it is mastered by the students, and then moves on to something new, this "organic" approach to teaching touches lightly on philosophical concepts in the beginning and then slowly builds a deeper understanding of the same concepts as they relate to recurrent motifs (p. 82).

In his discussion of the improvement of moral judgment, Lipman states that "the net pedagogical effect of stage theory is to confuse and misguide teachers rather than illuminate them as to the proper role they may assume in moral guidance of their students" (p. 184).

A general conceptualization of the nature of intelligence is offered by Lipman from the perspective of thinking skills and their relationship to basic skills. He describes the thinking process as a "vast and intricate family of activities," which include mathematical, historical, practical, and poetical thinking, as well as the kinds of thinking one does during such activities as reading, writing, dancing, playing, and speaking. According to Lipman,

Reading and mathematics are sometimes called the "basic skills" because they are said to be able to unlock and to

*reinforce other cognitive skills. But reading and mathe-
matics are simply two expressions of cognitive processing;
performance in these areas can be no better than the thinking skills that underlie them. From an educational point
of view, the improvement of thinking skills is of crucial and
foundational importance* (p. 16).

Theoretical Bases Compared

In a discussion of Feuerstein's instrumental and Sternberg's
componential approaches to the training of intelligence, Sternberg (1984) analyzes the differences and similarities of the
underlying theoretical bases. He indicates that they both
emphasize information processing and the training of intelligent thinking and behavior and that they both perceive intelligence as a dynamic entity, unlike the static factorial (psychometric) model, which cannot capture all that intelligence
is about. Sternberg, however, sees Feuerstein's construct as
having too many discrete parts, which he says overlap and
interact to process information. Feuerstein's theory of intelligence is said to be componential, while Sternberg's theory
is based on the concept of metacomponential performance.

The more specific comparisons made by Sternberg indicate
that he perceives his taxonomy as tighter, more succinct. He
characterizes Feuerstein's components as representing a broad
range of functions, while he considers his metacomponential
structure to be one that classifies processes according to the
functions they serve. Sternberg acknowledges Feuerstein's
use of noncognitive elements, such as motivation, while he
uses none. Thus, the theories have different implications for
the kinds of training that should be used to enhance intelligence performance.

Sternberg (1984) perceives his theory as one that implies
detailed process training with emphasis on transferability of
the process trained, such as the crystallized ability to derive
meanings of words from contexts. Transferability of Feuerstein's training has been more widely questioned in terms
of the relativity of his visual/spatial symbol tasks to such areas
as reading comprehension and oral and written expression,
although both theories show concern for generalizability as
well as durability by building in assessments for these con-
siderations. Finally, Sternberg indicates that group implementation of both training programs would result in the loss of
necessary individualization. Thus, both programs would be

more suitable for a one-on-one context in the developmental laboratory setting.

In another discussion of understanding and increasing intelligence, Sternberg (1984) compares Feuerstein's instrumental approach to Lipman's philosophical approach. He indicates that whereas Feuerstein's program minimizes the need for a knowledge base (experiential background), the philosophical approach draws greatly on the need for a knowledge base. Whereas Feuerstein's training approach minimizes the verbal load in problem solving, Lipman's approach relies on a heavy verbal load because the philosophical program emphasizes class discussion. (It would seem that Lipman's verbal approach would have more transferability than Feuerstein's visual/spatial approach.) Finally, whereas Feuerstein's instrumental approach is considered more appropriate for individuals with low-level abilities, Lipman's philosophical approach is said to be more appropriate for those with higher levels of abilities.

Sternberg, Feuerstein, and Lipman, proponents of three different approaches to the development of intelligence, each advocate a theory and/or program of training that has been widely implemented and indicative of success in varying aspects—verbal comprehension, visual/spatial problem solving, and the logic of discussion. It would seem that where these models do not overlap but do yield success in response to their specific focus, the most timely instructional programs would seek to adapt the most positive elements from each and utilize them when deemed specifically appropriate for the particular student.

Relativity of Current Theory to Developmental Studies

Developmental programs need to deliver instruction of the utmost integrity in terms of purpose, content, and scope. Such programs should provide developmental/remedial instruction to all individuals seeking postsecondary education who demonstrate interest, effort, and persistence in pursuing further education and who are in need of improvement in any of the basic skills areas. This instruction should seek to develop undeveloped abilities, remediate difficulties in the individual's learning processes, and assist students in replacing poor study habits with effective study habits. Such programs should also embody a content that will optimize the learning experience for the student by using methods and materials that challenge and provoke curiosity and are also in congruence with the student's general ability level, specific strengths and weaknesses, and the particular sociocultural identity.

Finally, the scope of such programs should include all aspects of instruction that contribute to successful study at the college level. Emphasis should be placed not only on the fundamentals of the basic skills areas, but also on a diverse spectrum of information, including that which is classic, contemporary, and futuristic. Students should be taught not only to understand and remember information, but also to question and criticize that which is stated and to infer and generate new information.

Ideally, developmental programs would offer instruction that incorporates aspects of Sternberg's approach to vocabulary and comprehension development, Feuerstein's approach to visual/spatial problem solving, and Lipman's approach to philosophical thought and discussion as an underlying framework for the enhancement of intelligence.

If we are concerned about the long-term success of students who progress through developmental studies and, subsequently, regular course offerings, then we must deliver the caliber of instruction, and allow the student the length of time, necessary to achieve a proficiency level beyond that required at the core course level. Indeed, students who initially enroll in developmental courses for the improvement of basic skills are, ultimately, in need of instruction that will develop their ability to engage in critical thinking and creative problem solving that can carry them beyond the basic skills exams and beyond core course levels.

Developmental students may also be in need of what Sternberg (1984) refers to as practical competence—strategies for successful interaction in the teaching/learning arena, such as appropriate turn-taking during class discussion or the appropriate prioritization of various assignments—ways in which the individual can successfully manipulate his or her abilities or demonstrate talents in order to attain further development.

If we seek to address the whole student, then programs should be both interdisciplinary, exemplifying the relativity of the basic skills areas to each other, and intercontextual, as conceptualized in Sternberg's "triarchic theory of intelligence," which refers to the internal underlying cognitive mechanisms, the external environmental aspects, and the experiential backgrounds of the individual. More succinctly, according to Sternberg (1984),

> *Before any program is adapted in a school curriculum, it should meet a set of basic prerequisites, such as: a) sound psychological and education foundations; b) socio-cultural appropriateness; c) responsiveness to motivational as well as cognitive needs, and d) the existence of links between the training and real-world behavioral requirements* (p. 11).

In keeping with the parameters of teaching and learning that are embodied in the efforts of Sternberg, Feuerstein, and Lipman, developmental programs should also strive to deliver the type of instruction that encompasses topics related to the services that many auxiliary intervention programs usually aim to address. While emphasizing the improvement of intelligence through practice in the areas of verbal comprehension, visual/spatial relationships, and philosophical thought, developmental programs would do much to optimize the effectiveness and value of curriculum and instruction by incorporating content directed toward student needs in the areas of personal health, self-awareness, interpersonal relations, career development, personal finance, and consumerism.

Individuals are better able to optimize their capabilities when they feel they can exert control over themselves and their environment. Programs of honest intent and integrity can afford to make a sincere effort to imbue students with a sense of self-worth and integrity by acknowledging their cultures, philosophies, and milieus in all that the curriculum imparts. Students need to perceive in their education some of the best of that which is characteristic of themselves so that they can perceive themselves as having a positive place in the world, for which the educational system professes to prepare its student body.

POLICY AND POSSIBILITIES FOR
FUTURE DEVELOPMENTAL PROGRAMS

The 1980s have been a period of great change in our educational outlook. Long-standing policies have been revamped and educational reform has been considered from many perspectives. New precollege curriculum requirements and new admissions and placement standards will be the primary factors that influence the administration of developmental programs. Public policy and its capacity to address the role of institutions of higher education, new trends in college curriculum, and the preparation of teachers and administrators will also have significant impact on the future directions of postsecondary developmental programs. Trends in the transition of students from high school to college will be a critical influence on program implementation.

New precollege curriculum requirements and new admissions and placement standards will be the primary factors that influence the administration of developmental programs.

   A variety of new directions in public policy have been suggested for the provision of remediation by all educational segments. In California, for example, four actions pertaining to the remedial education of skill-deficient adults have been proposed to the Board of Governors of the California Community College. The intent of the proposal is to generate cohesion in remediation policy. Its components are as follows (Farland 1985):

1. That the Board of Governors approve a definition of remediation that identifies purposes and course levels and endorse modification of course classifications to create consistency with the definition.
2. That the board direct staff to develop guidelines for determining which levels of instruction in English as a second language are equivalent to standards applied in English for remedial instruction.
3. That the Board should continue to seek legislation to authorize the implementation, funding, and evaluation of matriculation.
4. That areas are identified in which there will be a major initiative for establishing public policy for the provision of remedial instruction and services.

Additional emphasis has also been placed on the role of the board in policymaking which would eliminate the awarding of degree credit for remedial courses and give priority in matriculation funding to colleges that agree to participate in a state evaluation of remedial instruction. Consideration is also given to monitoring the improvement of high school preparation, interfacing with state universities, and delineating responsibility with the adult schools.

Focal points in policymaking should be influenced, to some extent, by the concerns expressed by developmental educators. Recent survey research indicates that faculty and administrators within institutions strongly identify with many concerns about developmental programs that would first appear to be external concerns. Although financial concerns and concerns for program quality, overall curricular integrity, and proper evaluation criteria represent policy issues for state agencies and the governing boards of public and private institutions, faculty and administrators also invest great interest in these areas (Clowes 1984a).

The Role of the State in Policy

It is essential that sound policies pertaining to developmental education be established at the state level, the predominant source from which a majority of postsecondary developmental programs receive financial support and governance. The following recommendations on the role of state governments in related policymaking have been selected from the literature because they seem the most timely, most aggressive, or most responsive to the future:

- States should facilitate the concept that the interdependence of all levels of education is critical and thus "seek to build an organizational and operational infrastructure that fosters cooperation, mutual respect, and creative interaction among educators and administrators throughout the system" (American Council on Education/Education Commission of the States 1988, p. 29).
- States should hold doctoral-granting and research institutions, including flagship universities, as equally responsible for strengthened developmental programs because "these institutions have sizeable enrollments and, although their percentages may be lower, the number of students affected could be higher than in many other state institutions of higher education" (Abraham 1988, p. 4).
- States should require that mandated statewide assessment and placement programs be established and be the same across all public institutions of higher education (Abraham 1988).
- States should authorize funding for developmental pro-

grams that will "at least be at a level commensurate with lower-division non-remedial courses and students" because such programs "can require comparatively greater efforts and costs" (Abraham 1988, p. 6).

- States should facilitate the implementation of interactive programs for high schools, two-year colleges, and four-year colleges, such as the Bridge Program model (Richards and Foster 1989), to bolster the success of high school graduates at risk.
- States should consider the establishment of relationships with private industry and other businesses that may bolster funding of developmental programs by enrolling their employees in need of developmental instruction (Mallery, Bullock, and Madden, 1987). At a time when college enrollments are decreasing in many systems, corporations may compete for prospective students by offering training and jobs simultaneously. Since technological and demographic change have resulted in fewer prepared individuals, corporations will assume the responsibility of training many workers that they cannot afford to wait for while they progress through traditional institutions of higher education (Nash and Hawthorne 1987).
- States should consider the establishment of links among postsecondary institutions, developmental programs, and other institutions (e.g., community centers, adult centers, and religious groups) in order to administer communication/literacy education more widely (Mallery, Bullock, and Madden 1987).
- States should support their institutions' developmental programs in the creation of courses for preparation in degree and technical areas in order to meet the needs of employed and nonemployed individuals in the non-traditional age range—this would help to reverse declining enrollment (Mallery, Bullock, and Madden 1987).
- States should set standards for the involvement of support services personnel in state and institutional decisions concerning admissions standards, assessment, and placement and in general policies related to academic assistance (Illinois Association for Personalized Learning Programs 1985).
- States should set standards that support communication and cooperation between vocational and developmental staff in their provision of services that develop the stu-

dents' job skills at the community-college level (Egbert 1985).

Since state interest in higher education will continue to shape the future context of independent higher education (Patillo and Redmon 1988), state government may also be instrumental in influencing policy of the independent institutions in response to the underprepared student. Possible actions taken by private institutions may include the following:

- restating the policy and philosophy undergirding admissions practices,
- challenging regional and national traditions in admissions,
- working with public and private schools and state systems to redefine the standards for moving from high school to college, and
- assisting high schools with efforts to prepare students for college-level work (Patillo and Redmon 1988, p. 4).

Despite the fact that public policy will inevitably affect developmental programs through the processes of top-level governing boards in ways perceived as both favorable and unfavorable, institutions and programs in some systems find satisfaction in the separation of policy and procedure. To the extent that procedures can now be changed in a program without necessarily requiring a change in policy, as was previously the case in many systems, the concept of policy is less of a deterrent to the flow of program administration and more of a resource for structure. Policy may make clear the need for meeting certain goals and objectives or satisfying certain requirements within set parameters. The institution or program may then decide to ensure its compliance by adapting procedures, such as involving the registrar's office in recordkeeping for the developmental department or creating a system of due process for developmental students, at its discretion. Thus, a balance between external policy and internal procedure can be achieved, hopefully to the ultimate benefit of those being served.

Although historical trends indicate that complete elimination of the problem of underprepared students is impossible, popular opinion does recognize the possibility of minimizing the extent of the problem. Concerned educators and administrators are advised to consider more rigorous high school curricula to reduce the number of underprepared students, better communication between high schools and colleges to aid students' transitions, and more carefully implemented remedial and developmental programs to increase the success rate of high-risk students (Ross and Roe 1986). In efforts to achieve a balance between equity and excellence, proponents suggest that major changes in faculty-load formulas and credit-hour funding would also do much to ensure equal access and quality (Cross 1983). The viability of a developmental studies program that is integrated into the total curriculum of the institution and that assists in integrating its students into the mainstream of its student population has been considered as another response to the pressures created by the equal access/academic standards dilemma (Clowes and Creamer 1979).

At the instructional level, trends and pressures also indicate the need for change. Developmental educators need to build on their flexibility and adaptability and to strive for professionalism. The needs of the nontraditional student should be given priority regarding program focus because program success is contingent on the effectiveness and efficiency of the program's effort to address those needs. Attention to professionalism is also critical because the importance of developmental programs is frequently minimized in comparisons with other academic programs. Professionalism will enhance the academic achievements of students and dispel misconceptions.

Training for Administrators and Faculty

Improvements in the professionalism of teachers and administrators of developmental programs will be given additional momentum by new developments in graduate training. Several doctoral programs in developmental education are now offered at various institutions across the nation. Most recently, attention has been directed to the expansion and refinement of these doctoral programs in terms of focus. Great emphasis has been placed on the need for stronger management training for individuals who will direct developmental and learning assistance programs (Keimig 1983; Maxwell 1980; J. Roueche and Baker 1986). A 1981 survey of learning assistance program staff members, for example, indicates that one of the top three

training priorities for such personnel was management development (Boylan 1981). In a statement issued by the National Council of Educational Opportunity Associations, the need for further development of management skills for those who direct programs for disadvantaged students was again recognized as a critical priority in higher education (Mitchem 1986).

More specifically, there has been recognition of a need for more training in the administration of developmental programs. Until very recently, only two institutions in the nation had established such graduate-level training—Appalachian State University in Boone, North Carolina, and Murray State University in Kentucky. Yet at the same time, over 40,000 people were involved in developmental education and learning assistance programs serving approximately 3 million students across the United States (Boylan 1985).

Recently, Grambling State University submitted a proposal for a doctor of education degree in developmental education, which included the following specifications: curriculum and instruction, student development and personnel services, instructional design and technology, and higher education administration. The Board of Regents of Louisiana approved the first three areas of specialization in 1986 but rejected the specialization in administration because of low interest and insufficient faculty available to instruct in this area. Since then, the decision on an administrative specialization has been reversed. Due to substantial numbers of applicants expressing interest in the administrative focus, an increase of faculty with expertise in the administration of developmental programs, and communication from college systems indicating interest in enrolling their middle-management personnel in the doctoral program if a degree track in administration became available, the proposal for an administrative specialization was finally accepted.

The expansion and refinement of related graduate programs are also exemplified by Grambling's recent establishment of a visiting scholar's program designed to bring some of the nation's leading researchers and practitioners in developmental education to teach in their doctoral program, and by the establishment of a research-in-residence program to bring additional individuals involved in developmental education research to the campus to use research facilities and interact with faculty and students. Grambling has recently set up a special arrangement with Hunter College of the City University of New York whereby Hunter will allow faculty members time off to meet the residency and other requirements of the doctoral degree. Over a three-year period, 30 Hunter faculty members will participate in the degree program. Similar arrangements are also being negotiated with other universities (Joiner 1988).

The effects of improved teacher and administrator professionalism that should be generated within developmental programs as a result of renewed policy, planning, and implementation strategies should become evident gradually. The preparedness of educators and administrators of developmental education can be continuously measured, to some extent, by the effectiveness of programs. Ultimately, however, program trends will still be affected largely by the nature and changes of student populations. Student preparedness, as measured in terms of transitions from high school to college, will remain a primary factor in determining the future directions of postsecondary developmental programs.

The Prospective Developmental Student Population

Data on the percentage of freshman enrolled in remedial subjects, recently included in *Indicators of Educational Status and Trends* (U.S. Department of Education 1985), indicate the importance of monitoring change in this profile and the need to determine the reasons for any change as a function of the percentage of high school graduates attending college, the adequacy of high school preparation, student aptitude, student choice of college, college entrance standards, the rigor of entry-level courses, and the availability of remedial courses (Wright and Cahalan 1985). More research will also be needed to delineate the types of students who enter developmental courses and the curriculum and instructional modes best suited to different groups of students, as well as the success rate of developmental students in degree programs (Morgan 1988).

A report of the Commission on Minority Participation in Education and the American Life, entitled *One Third of a Nation,* predicts that "between 1985 and 2000, minority workers will make up one-third of the net additions to the U.S. labor force" and that "by the year 2000, almost 42 percent of all public school students will be minority children or other children in poverty" (American Council on Education/ Education Commission of the States 1988, p. 2). Perhaps these projections hold implications for an even greater increase in the diversity of the prospective developmental student population (the projected one-third minority is said to consist mainly of African-Americans, Hispanics, and Native Americans). That population will consist of many nonminority individuals, however, as evidenced in economic forecasts of the state of the nation. In an exhaustive analysis of the economic performance of our country during the 1980s, Peterson (1987, p. 60) reemphasizes a conclusion of the 1983 National Commission on Excellence in Education: "for the first time in the history of our country, the educational skills for one generation will not surpass, will not equal, will not even approach, those of their parents." No doubt this statement holds implications for nonminorities because, to date, minority youths continue to exceed their parents' educational achievement levels for the aggregate (see also section 2).

In some systems, future changes in the profile of the developmental student population will, no doubt, be a function of recent changes in policy related to efforts to improve quality. In some cases, the upgrading of college-level work will affect the number of students enrolling in developmental programs. The recent requirement of higher SAT scores to avoid developmental courses will also affect the profile. In the University System of Georgia, for example, lower-division math courses outside of the core curriculum have been upgraded, required SAT scores have been raised, and the long-used Basic Skills Exam has been replaced by the new College Placement Exam, which has higher minimum standards— all expected to lead to an increase in the enrollment of developmental students. These policy changes have been generated, in part, by the Quality Basic Education (QBE) Act for educational reform, which was initiated in 1983 and has not yet been fully implemented. The first high school students required to meet the QBE requirements will graduate in 1989. They will then be faced with new college admission and placement standards, which will inevitably create new profiles in the developmental program population.

Ironically, although institutions of higher education whose primary mission is research, or a combination of research and teaching, are most likely to be opposed to the existence or expansion of developmental programs on their campuses, the recent declines in student enrollment and the raising of admissions standards will probably create the need for these same institutions to establish, expand, or improve developmental programs. With their low priority on teaching, these institutions tend to be more in danger of higher student attrition rates due to mismatches between student competency and faculty expectations. In many instances, the more that emphasis is placed on research, the less the effort faculty place on refining pedagogical skills and the more often beginning students lose in the educational process. In other instances, students may be subject to the common misfortune of having an instructor who is the "cream of the crop" in research expertise but who teaches above the heads of the class. The literature indicates that approximately one-third of institutions of higher education that do operate a developmental program are institutions whose primary mission is not teaching. Clearly, these institutions and those that have no learning assistance program may need to reassess the value of such programs to their future success.

The General Prosperity of Programs

A substantial number of institutions that have developmental programs have selective rather than open admissions policies. As mentioned previously, faculty who are involuntarily assigned to teach remedial/developmental courses and those who generally support the notion that such courses dilute the academic integrity of the institution can often create a major deterrent to the prosperity of the developmental program. In some cases, faculty and staff who may have negative attitudes about the value of the program may also create deterrents to obtaining objective and accurate information on internal program evaluations. Where significant levels of resistance are identified, administrators should respond to possible recalcitrance by conducting sensitivity workshops.

In approximately 50 percent of postsecondary institutions conducting learning assistance programs, the programs are separately or jointly administered. Some programs, for example, operate as a separate entity, not belonging to any other school or college or any other division on their campus; they report directly to the Office of Academic Affairs, the Office of Student Affairs, or some combination of offices. Considering issues of recognition, relativity of curriculum, and prosperity, it may be prudent for some of these programs to become centralized. Academic recognition and relativity may be facilitated when developmental faculty are incorporated into a standing department or school, thereby increasing their opportunities for joint research and curriculum development with other experts in their field. Programs may also be enhanced if centralization obtains more substantial line-item funding. (The primary sources of funding for a majority of programs are university line items, federal funds, and academic department funds.)

Developmental Research
Another area for future focus is the importance of developmental research, which is currently acknowledged by a majority of learning assistance programs, within which staff conduct their own research. Surprisingly, however, a substantial number of programs conduct very little in-house research. Although the literature provides reputable and continuous sources of research on a variety of topics and issues germane to teaching and learning for remedial/developmental populations, in programs in which developmental practitioners are not guided by their own research, there is more room for the possible deterioration of effectiveness. Staff should be encouraged to conduct their own research, and administrators should provide the support necessary for such endeavors. In terms of research for program evaluation, many institutions indicate that they assess their program effectiveness on the basis of a variety of measures, including the frequency of student attendance in nonmandatory programs, the responses given in student evaluations of the program, top-level administrative office assessments and feedback, and students' performance and persistence in the program and beyond the program.

Future focus should, advisedly, be placed particularly on the grade point average as an indicator of program effectiveness. The literature indicates that the grade point average is more defensible than any other measure of program effectiveness. It is a more accurate measure and predictor of student performance—even more so than standardized test scores (Vines 1988) and student performance is the ultimate measure of program success. (Standardized tests, to some extent, measure only performance on the test, but the grade point average is an indicator of performance at a variety of tasks over a substantial span of time.) It should also be noted that, since numerous programs are based solely on the objective of preparing students for the core curriculum (mainly freshman courses), such programs would do more justice to evaluations of effectiveness by using comparisons of grade point average up to and including only the first year of matriculation.

There is very little indication of external program evaluation in the literature. Perhaps, in the struggle to achieve a balance between equity and excellence, programs at all points on the continuum of failure to success would do well to undergo evaluation by external agencies. It is likely that external evaluation has not been considered frequently in order to protect the developmental department that is often perceived as a "stepchild" from being evaluated as a "stepchild." The concept of accountability, often associated with evaluation, has created negative connotations in education when administrators and faculty are made to feel responsible for program and student outcomes, which can easily be hampered by uncontrollable variables. However, if sound evaluation procedures are identified—in terms of utility, timeliness, participant ownership of data, and cost effectiveness—and those procedures are used with objectivity, then administrators and practitioners may enhance their ability to make informed and unbiased decisions about the improvement and direction of developmental programs for the future. The option of external evaluation will probably be best received by potential participants when the evaluator is independent of federal funding offices or boards that apply political pressure in order to obtain funds, satisfy governing offices, or maintain public confidence.

REFERENCES

The Educational Resources Information Center (ERIC) Clearinghouse
on Higher Education abstracts and indexes the current literature
on higher education for inclusion in ERIC's data base and announce-
ment in ERIC's monthly bibliographic journal, *Resources in Education* (RIE). Many of these publications are available through the
ERIC Document Reproduction Service (EDRS). For publications
cited in this bibliography that are available from EDRS, ordering
number and price code are included. Readers who wish to order
a publication should write to the ERIC Document Reproduction
Service, 3900 Wheeler Avenue, Alexandria, Virginia 22304. (Phone
orders with VISA or MasterCard are taken at 800/227-ERIC or 703/
823-0500.) When ordering, please specify the document (ED) number. Documents are available as noted in microfiche (MF) and paper
copy (PC). If you have the price code ready when you call EDRS,
an exact price can be quoted. The last page of the latest issue of
Resources in Education also has the current cost, listed by code.

Abraham, A. 1986. "College-level Study: What Is It?" *Issues in Higher
Education,* Southern Regional Education Board, No. 22.
———. 1987. *Placement and Retention in Remedial/Developmental
Programs in the SREB States.* Atlanta, Ga.: Southern Regional Edu-
cation Board.
———. 1988. "Remedial Education in College: How Widespread
Is It?" *Issues in Higher Education,* Southern Regional Education
Board, No. 24
Ahrendt, K.M. 1975. *Community College Reading Programs.* Newark,
Del.: International Reading Association.
Akst, G., and Hecht, M. 1980. "Program Evaluation." In A.S. Trillin
and Associates, *Teaching Basic Skills in College.* San Francisco:
Jossey-Bass.
Albright, B.T. 1927. "Typical Reading Disabilities of College Entrants."
Master's thesis, University of Southern California.
Algier, A.S. 1972. "A New Approach to Academic Rehabilitation."
Educational Record 53: 80-84.
American Council on Education and the Education Commission
of the States. 1988. *One-third of a Nation.* The Commission on
Minority Participation in Education and American Life. Washington,
D.C.: American Council on Education and the Education Com-
mission of the States.
American Association of Higher Education-ERIC. 1981. *Functional
Literacy in the College Setting.* Higher Education Research Report
No. 3. Washington, D.C.: American Association of Higher Edu-
cation. ED 211 032. 52 pp. MF–01; PC–03.
Astin, A.W. 1971. "Open Admissions and Programs for the Disad-
vantaged." Paper presented at National Conference on Higher
Education, Chicago. ED 050 692. 18 pp. MF–01; PC–01.

————. 1975. *Preventing Students from Dropping Out*. San Francisco: Jossey-Bass.

Astin, H.S.; Astin, A.W.; Bisconti, A.S.; and Frankel, H.H. 1972. *Higher Education and the Disadvantaged Student*. Washington, D.C.: Human Service Press. (*College Student Personnel Abstracts*, 1973, 8(2): 275-276.)

————. 1985. "Providing Incentives for Teaching Underprepared Students." *Educational Record* 66: 26–29.

Bailey, J.L. 1982. "An Evaluation of Journal Published Research of College Reading Study Skills, 1925-1980." Ph.D. dissertation, University of Tennessee.

Bass, R. 1982. *Junior College Articulation: Admission, Retention, Remediation, Transfer*. Position Paper. College Park: University of Maryland. ED 231 484. 17 pp. MF–01; PC–01.

Belcher, M.J. 1971. "The Effect of Increased Reading Efficiency upon Semester Grade Point Average." *Journal of Reading* 14: 381. (*College Student Personnel Abstracts*, 1972, 7(4): 489–490.)

Bers, T.H. 1987. *Evaluating Remedial Education Programs*. Association for Institutional Research Professional File. Tallahassee: Association for Institutional Research. ED 282 492. 9 pp. MF–01; PC–01.

Blake, W.S. 1953. "A Survey and Evaluation of Study Skills Programs at the College Level in the United States and Possessions." Ph.D. dissertation, University of Maryland.

Bloom, B.S. 1956. *Taxonomy of Educational Objectives: The Classification of Educational Goals*. New York: Longmans, Green.

————. 1971. "Mastery Learning." In *Mastery Learning: Theory and Practice*, edited by J.H. Block. New York: Holt, Rinehart, & Winston.

Book, W.F. 1927. "Results Obtained in a Special "How to Study" Course Given to College Students." *School and Society* 26: 529–534.

Boylan, H.R. 1981. "Survey of Training Needs among Learning Assistance Program Personnel." Paper presented at the American College Personnel Association Convention, Boston.

————. 1985. "Academic Achievement Trends among Disadvantaged Youth." *Research in Developmental Education* 2: 1.

Brody, L.; Harris, B.; and Lachica, G. 1968. *Discovering and Developing the College Potential of Disadvantaged High School Youth: A Report of the Second Year of a Longitudinal Study of the College Discovery and Development Program*. New York: Office of Research and Evaluation, City University of New York. ED 034 809. 211 pp. MF–01; PC–09.

Brown, A.L. 1978. "Knowing When, Where, and How to Remember: A Problem of Metacognition." In *Advances in Instructional Psychology*, edited by R. Glaser. Hillsdale, N.J.: Erlbaum.

Brown, W.F. 1971. "Effect of Student to Student Counseling on the Academic Adjustment of Potential College Dropouts." *Journal of Educational Psychology* 2: 285–289.

Broyles, S.G. 1982. *Fall Enrollment in Colleges and Universities, 1982.* Higher Education General Information System. Washington, D.C.: National Center for Education Statistics.

Bucklin, R., and Bucklin, M. 1971. "A Program to Assist Marginal College Freshmen." *Journal of the National Association of Women Deans and Counselors* 34: 148–150.

Budig, J.E. 1986. "An Evaluation of a Junior College Developmental Education Program." *AIR 1986 Annual Forum Paper.* Indianapolis, Ind.: Association for Institutional Research. ED 280 393. 22 pp. MF–01; PC–01.

Buswell, G.T. 1939. *Remedial Reading at the College and Adult Levels: An Experimental Study.* Supplementary Educational Monographs, No. 50. Chicago: University of Chicago Press.

Campbell, R. 1982. *Developmental and Remedial Education: A Survey of AATC American Association of Community and Junior College Members, 1981.* ED 221 247. 16 pp. MF–01; PC–01.

Christ, F.L. 1971. "Systems for Learning Assistance: Learners, Learning Facilitators, and Learning Centers." *Interdisciplinary Aspects of Reading Instruction,* edited by F. L. Christ. Proceedings of the Fourth Annual Conference of the Western College Reading Association, Los Angeles. ED 114 795. 159 pp. MF–01; PC–07.

Clowes, D.A. 1984a. "Critical Issues Facing Developmental Education: A Survey." *A Compendium of Up-to-Date Research on Topics Ranging from Software to Program Evaluation.* National Association for Developmental Research, Report No. 3. ED 274 382. 78 pp. MF–01; PC–04.

———. 1984b. "The Evaluation of Remedial/Developmental Programs: A Stage Model of Program Evaluation. *Journal of Developmental Education* 8: 1ff.

L Clowes, D.A., and Creamer, D. 1979. "From Differentiation to Integration: Curricular Patterns in Developmental/Remedial Studies." Southern Studies. *College Personnel Association Journal* 2: 1ff.

College Board Educational Equality Project. 1983. *Academic Preparation for College: What Students Need to Know and Be Able to Do.* New York: Office of Academic Affairs. The College Board. ED 232 517. 53 pp. MF–01; PC not avail. EDRS.

Cross, K.P. 1976. *Accent on Learning.* San Francisco: Jossey-Bass.

———. 1981. *Adults as Learners.* San Francisco: Jossey-Bass.

———. 1983. *Underprepared Learners.* Current Issues in Higher Education, 1, 1982-1983. Washington, D.C.: American Association for Higher Education. ED 233 636. 35 pp. MF–01; PC–02.

Davis, J.A.; Burkheimer, G.,; and Borders-Patterson, A. 1975. *The Impact of Special Services Programs in Higher Education for Dis-*

advantaged Students. Princeton, N.J.: Educational Testing Service. ED 112 790. 589 pp. MF–01; PC–24.

Dempsey, J.L. 1978. *An Update on the Organization and Administration of Learning Assistance Programs in U.S. Senior Institutions of Higher Education.* ED 257 334. 52 pp. MF–01; PC–03.

Dickens, M.E. 1980. *Competencies for Developmental Educators.*2nd ed. _____, S.C.: Instructional ACCtion Center. ED 203 909. 56 pp. MF–01; PC–03.

DiSalvi, R.D. 1971. "A Remedial Program for Undergraduate Evening Students." *Adult Education* 21: 186–195.

Dunbar, W. 1935. "Public versus Private Control of Higher Education in Michigan, 1817-1855." *Mississippi Valley Historical Review* 22: 390–392.

Dunphy, L.; Miller, T.E.; Woodruff, T.; and Nelson, J.E. 1989. "Freshman Seminars: A Retention Tool at Trenton State College." *The Freshman Year Experience Newsletter,* University of South Carolina, I(1): 6.

Egbert, M. 1985. "Building Bridges: Vocational Educators and Developmental Education Techniques." *Lifelong Learning* 8(8): 29–30. ED 272 659. 3 pp. MF–01; PC–01.

Egerton, J. 1968. *Higher Education for "High Risk" Students.* Atlanta, Ga.: Southern Education Reporting Service, Southern Education Foundation. ED 023 745. 60 pp. MF–01; PC–03.

Enright, G. 1975. *College Learning Skills: Frontierland Origins of the Learning Assistance Center.* Proceedings of the Eighth Annual Conference of the Western College Reading Association. Las Cruces, N.M.: Western College Reading Association. ED 105 424. 20 pp. MF–01; PC–01.

Erickson, M.E., and Rosica, A.D. 1978. "Developmental Courses Are Creditable." *Community College Frontiers,* Spring, 6: 19.

Ervin, L., and Tomlinson, L. 1986. *Implications of the New Criteria for Developmental Studies.* Athens, Ga.: Institute of Higher Education. ED 277 303. 6 pp. MF–01; PC–01.

Farland, R.W. 1985. *Proposals for Board Policies and Actions Concerning Remediation in the California Community Colleges.* Sacramento: California Community Colleges, Office of the Chancellor. ED 256 433. 7 pp. MF–01; PC–01.

Ferrin, R.I. 1971. "Developmental Programs in Midwestern Community Colleges." *College Entrance Examination Board Higher Education Survey.* Report No. 4. (*College Student Personnel Abstracts,* 1972, 7(2): 229.)

Feuerstein, R. 1980. *Instrumental Enrichment: An Intervention Program for Cognitive Modifiability.* Baltimore, Md.: University Park Press.

Flavell, J.H. 1976. "Metacognitive Aspects of Problem Solving." In *The Nature of Intelligence,* edited by L.B. Resnick. New York: John

Wiley & Sons.

Friedlander, J. 1981. "Should Remediation Be Mandatory?" *Community College Review,* 9: 3ff.

—————. 1984. "Delivering Academic Assistance: Exemplary Approaches." *Journal of Developmental and Remedial Education* 7 (Spring): 13–15ff.

Gattman, E. 1967. "College? Man, You Must Be Kidding." *NEA Journal,* pp. 8–10.

Glass, G. 1976. "Primary, Secondary, and Meta-analysis of Research." *Educational Research* 5: 3–8.

Gordon, E. 1970. "Programs and Practices for Minority Group Youth in Higher Education." In *Barriers to Higher Education: A College Entrance Examination Board Colloquium. New York: College Entrance Examination Board. (College Student Personnel Abstracts,* 288–289.)

—————. 1971. "Equality of Educational Opportunity—Is It Possible in Our Lifetime?" Paper presented at the annual meeting of the National Association of Human Rights Workers.

Gordon, E.W., and Wilkerson, D.A. 1966. *Compensatory Education for the Disadvantaged—Programs and Practices: Pre-school Through College.* New York: College Entrance Examination Board.

Haggerty, M.E., and Eurich, A.C. 1929. *A Test of Reading Comprehension.* Minneapolis: University of Minnesota.

Hardesty 1986. *Coordinating Board of the Texas College and University System Newsletter* 86: 1.

Herscher, B.R. 1980. "Competency-based Education: A Viable Alternative for Developmental Studies Program Design." *Journal of Developmental and Remedial Education* 4: 1ff.

Higher Education Opportunity Program. 1970. *Report to the Legislature.* Albany: State Education Department of the State of New York. ED 043 304. 27 pp. MF–01; PC–02.

Huey, E. 1969. *The Psychology and Pedagogy of Reading.* 1908. Cambridge, Mass: MIT Press.

Human Affairs Research Center. 1970. *The Expansion of Equal Education Opportunities: An Evaluation Study of the New York State Higher Education Opportunity Program.* Albany: State Education Department of the State of New York. ED 051 763. 49 pp. MF–01; PC–02.

Illinois Association for Personalized Learning Programs. 1985. *The Role of Developmental Education Programs in Providing Educational Excellence.* Illinois Association for Personalized Learning Programs. ED 258 605. 12 pp. MF–01; PC–01.

Joiner, B. 1988. "Grambling Initiates Developmental Ph.D. Program: Unique Degree Fills Educational Void." *Black Issues in Higher Education* 4: 22.

Jones, G.P. 1984. "The Tutor as Counselor." *Journal of Develop-*

mental Education 8(1): 12ff.

Joplin, A., and Brown, A. 1981. *Is There Any Difference? A Comparative Study of Developmental Reading Programs in Traditional Black Colleges and Universities and Their White Counterparts for the 1979-80 Academic Year.* St. Louis, Mo. ED 202 417. 51 pp. MF–01; PC not avail. EDRS.

Kaye, R.A. 1972. "A Required Counseling-Study Skills Program for Failing College Freshmen." *Journal of College Student Personnel* 13: 159–162.

Keimig, R.T. 1983. *Raising Academic Standards: A Guide to Learning Improvement.* ASHE-ERIC Higher Education Research Report No. 4. Washington, D.C.: Association for the Study of Higher Education. ED 233 669. 100 pp. MF–01; PC–04.

Kersteins, G. 1971. *Junior-Community College Reading/Study Skills.* Newark, Del.: International Reading Association.

Kling, M. 1972. "Summer Head Start for Disadvantaged College Freshmen." *Journal of Reading* 15: 507–515.

Klingelhofer, E.L., and Longacre, B.J. 1972. "A Case in Point." *Research Reporter* 7(3): 5–8.

Kulik, C.C.; Kulik, J.A.; and Schwalb, B.J. 1983. "College Programs for High-Risk and Disadvantaged Students: A Meta-analysis of Findings." *Review of Educational Research* 53: 397–414.

Leedy, P.D. 1958. "A History of the Origin and Development of Instruction in Reading Improvement at the College Level." Ph.D. dissertation, New York University.

———. 1964. *College-Adult Reading Instruction.* Newark, Del.: International Reading Association.

Lipman, M. 1980. *Philosophy in the Classroom.* Philadelphia: Temple University Press.

Lombardi, J. 1979. "Four Phases of Developmental Education." *Junior College Resource Review.* Los Angeles: University of California and ERIC Clearinghouse for Junior College Information. ED 165 858. 6 pp. MF–01; PC–01.

Lowe, A.J. 1966. *Surveys of College Reading Improvement Programs— 1929-1966.* ED 011 230. 14 pp. MF–01; PC–01.

———. 1970. *The Rise of College Reading, the Good and Bad and the Indifferent—1915-1970.* ED 040 013. 14 pp. MF–01; PC–01.

Mallery, A.; Bullock, T.L.; and Madden, D.A. 1987. "Future Trends in College Developmental Reading Programs." Paper presented at the American Reading Forum, Sarasota, Florida.

Marshall, J.S. 1981. *A Model for Improving the Retention and Academic Achievement of Non-traditional Students at Livingston College/Rutgers University.* New Brunswick, N.J.: Rutgers University. ED 203 831. 34 pp. MF–01; PC–02.

Maxwell, M. 1980. *Improving Student Learning Skills.* San Francisco: Jossey-Bass.

Menges, R.J.; Max, R.; and Trumpeter, P.W. 1972. "Effectiveness of Tutorial Assistance for High-Risk Students in Advanced College Courses." *Journal of Counseling Psychology* 19: 229- 233.

Miller, M.B. 1984. "Developmental Education and Speech Communication in the Community College." *Communication Education* 33: 1ff.

Mitchem, A. 1986. Personal conversation at the National Conference on Exemplary Programs in Developmental Education, Atlanta.

Moore, W. 1971. *Blind Man on a Freeway: The Community College Administrator.* London: Jossey-Bass.

———. 1984. *Summary of Review Conference.* Report on Interview with Bert C. Bach. Columbus: Ohio State University.

Morgan, D. 1988. "Dispelling False Notions." *Systems,* University System of Georgia, 24: 5.

Nash, N.S., and Hawthorne, E.M. 1987. *Formal Recognition of Employer-Sponsored Instruction: Conflict and Collegiality in Postsecondary Education.* ASHE-ERIC Higher Education Report No. 3. Washington, D.C.: Association for the Study of Higher Education. ED 286 437. 128 pp. MF–01; PC–06.

Norlander, K.A., and Anderson, P. 1987. "Instructional Alternatives for College Students with Learning Disabilities: Remediation or Compensation." Paper presented at the American Reading Forum, Sarasota, Florida.

Oskamp, S.; Hodges, P.F.; Thompson, K.S.; and Spuck, D. 1970. "Effects of a Compensatory College Education Program for the Disadvantaged: A Further Report." Paper presented at meeting of the Western Psychological Association, Los Angeles. ED 041 973. 8 pp. MF–01; PC–01.

Parr, F.W. 1930. "The Extent of Remedial Work in State Universities in the United States." *School and Society* 31: 547–548.

Patillo, M., and Redmon, E.R. 1988. "Imperatives for Private Higher Education: Serving the Public Interest." Paper presented at the Invitational Seminar on Planning Imperatives for the 1990s, Institute of Higher Education, Georgia Center for Continuing Education, Athens.

Pauk, W. 1962. *How to Study in College.* Boston: Houghton Mifflin.

Perry, W.G. 1959. "Students' Use and Misuse of Reading Skills: A Report to a Faculty." *Harvard Educational Review* 29: 193–200.

Peterson, P.G. 1987. "The Morning After." *Atlanta Monthly* 260(4): 43–69.

Remmers, H.H. 1927. "A Diagnostic and Remedial Study of Potentially and Actually Failing Students at Purdue University." Ph.D. dissertation, University of Iowa.

Richards, W., and Foster, J.M. 1989. "The Bridge Program: Successful Collaboration among High Schools, a Community College and a Four-year College." Paper presented at the National Association for Developmental Education, 13th Annual Conference, Cincinnati.

Roberts, G.H. 1986. *Developmental Education: An Historical Study.* ED 276 395. 23 pp. MF–01; PC–01.

Robinson, F.P. 1933. *The Role of Eye-Movements in Reading with an Evaluation of Techniques for their Improvement.* Series on Aims and Progress of Research, No. 39. Iowa City: Iowa State University.

Ross, E.P., and Roe, B.D. 1986. *The Case for Basic Skills Programs in Higher Education.* Fastback 238. Bloomington, Ind.: Phi Delta Kappa. ED 273 166. 43 pp. MF–01; PC–02.

Roueche, J.E. 1984. *Between a Rock and a Hard Place.* Washington, D.C.: National Conference on Adult Literacy.

Roueche, J.E., and Baker, G. 1986. *College Responses to Low-achieving Students.* New York: Harcourt Brace & Jovanovich.

Roueche, J.E., and Snow, J. 1977. *Overcoming Learning Problems.* San Francisco: Jossey-Bass.

Roueche, J.E.; Baker, G.A., III; and Roueche, S.D. 1984. *College Responses to Low-achieving Students: A National Study.* Orlando. Fla.: HBJ Media Systems.

Roueche, S.D. 1983. "Elements of Program Success: Report of a National Study." In *A New Look at Successful Programs,* edited by John Roueche. San Francisco: Jossey-Bass.

Sanders, V.A. 1979. "A Meta-analysis: The Relationship of Program Content and Operation Factors to Measured Effectiveness of College Reading Study." Ph.D. dissertation, University of the Pacific.

Schmelzer, R., and Brozo, W.G. 1982. "A Skills Therapy Approach for Developmental Learning in College." *Journal of Reading* 25 (April): 646–655.

Sharma, S.C. 1977. *Academic Support Services Programs in Higher Education.* Whitewater: University of Wisconsin. ED 221 079. 73 pp. MF 01; PC not avail. EDRS.

Simmons, W.D. 1970. *Survey and Analysis of Higher Education Programs for the Disadvantaged Student.* Washington, D.C.: Department of Health, Education and Welfare. ED 040 262. 66 pp. MF–01; PC–03.

Southern Regional Education Board. 1971. *The College and Cultural Diversity: The Black Student on Campus: A Project Report.* Atlanta, Ga.: Southern Regional Education Board. ED 055 563. 86 pp. MF–01; PC–04.

Starks, G. 1982. *Efficiency in the 80's in Reading and Study Skills.* ED 222 861. 10 pp. MF–01; PC–01.

Sternberg, R.J. 1977. *Intelligence, Information Processing, and Analogical Reasoning: The Componential Analysis of Human Abilities.* Hillsdale, N.J.: Erlbaum.

———. 1983. *How Can We Teach Intelligence?* Philadelphia: Urban Development, Research for Better Schools, Inc.

————. 1984a. "Instrumental and Componential Approaches to the Training of Intelligence." In *Thinking and Learning Skills: Current Research and Open Questions,* edited by S. Chapman, J. Segal, and R. Glass. Vol. I. Hillsdale, N.J.: Erlbaum.

————. 1984b. *Understanding and Increasing Your Intelligence, Teacher's Guide.*

Tetlow, W.L. 1970. "Preliminary Investigations on the Academic Performance of Minority Group Students at Cornell University." Paper presented at meeting of American Association for the Advancement of Science, Chicago. ED 051 744. 16 pp. MF–01; PC–01.

Tomlinson, L. 1987. *Overview of Computer Applications in Reading.* ED 276 978. 46 pp. MF–01; PC–02.

————. 1985. *Group Oral Review in the Reading Lab: A Means of Synthesizing Individualized Approaches to One Body of Written Material.* ED 259 305. 11 pp. MF–01; PC–01.

"Toughening Up on Admissions." 1982. *Time,* January 11, pp. 72.

University System of Georgia. 1973. *A Plan for the Further Desegregation of the University System of Georgia.* OCR Report. Atlanta: University System of Georgia. ED 092 021. 244 pp. MF–01; PC–10.

————. 1984. *Response to Findings of the Office for Civil Rights.* The Regent's Test Program. Atlanta: University System of Georgia. ED 245 636. 21 pp. MF–01; PC–01.

Urban Problem Solving Program. 1970. *Report on Transitional Year 1969-70, College of Arts and Sciences.* Kansas City: University of Missouri. ED 049 673. 19 pp. MF–01; PC–01.

U.S. Department of Education. 1985. *Indicators of Educational Status and Trends.* Washington, D.C.: U.S. Department of Education.

U.S. Department of Health, Education and Welfare. 1970. *Special Services for Disadvantaged Students in Institutions of Higher Education Program: Application Information and Program Manual.* Washington, D.C.: Bureau of Higher Education. U.S. Department of Health, Education and Welfare. ED 040 658. 39 pp. MF–01; PC–02.

————. 1972. *Annual Evaluation Report on Education Programs: Fiscal Year.* Washington, D.C.: U.S. Department of Health, Education and Welfare. ED 082 300. 333 pp. MF–01; PC–14.

Vassar College. 1866. *Annual Report to the Board of Trustees.* Poughkeepsie, N.Y.: Vassar College.

Vines, D. 1988. "SAT Scores Distort Potential." *Recruitment and Retention in Higher Education* 2(1): 9.

Wenrich, J.W. 1971. *Keeping Dropouts In: Retention of Students Identified as High Probability Dropouts.* Washington, D.C.: U.S. Department of Health, Education and Welfare. ED 047 684. 32 pp. MF–01; PC–02.

Whimbey, A., and Lockhead, J. 1983. *Analytical Reading and Rea-*

soning. Stamford, Conn.: Innovative Sciences.

Wilkerson, D.A. 1966. "Compensatory Practices in Colleges and Universities." *Information Retrieval Center on the Disadvantaged Bulletin,* pp. 1-3. ED 011 908. 6 pp. MF–01; PC–01.

Wilson, R. 1970. *The Effects of Special Tutoring and Counseling on the Academic Success of Negro Freshmen at Southern State College: Final Report.* Washington, D.C.: U.S. Department of Health, Education and Welfare. ED 043 314. 107 pp. MF–01; PC–05.

Wright, D.A., and Cahalan, M.W. 1985. *Remedial/developmental Studies in Institutions of Higher Education: Policies and Practices.* Rockville, Md.: Westat Research. ED 263 828. 26 pp. MF–01; PC–02.

Yuthas, L.J. 1971. "Student Tutors in a College Remedial Program." *Journal of Reading* 14: 231. (*College Student Personnel Abstracts,* 1972, 7(4): 490–491.)

Zanoni, C. 1982. *1980-1981 General College Retention Program: Final Report.* Minneapolis: General College, University of Minnesota. ED 216 595. 156 pp. MF–01; PC–07.

INDEX

A

Academic recognition: lack of, 51
Access to education, 35
Adjunct courses, 25
Administrative support, 42
Administrator training, 77–79
Admission standards, 2,
      criteria, 17
      minimum, 44–45
      state action, 6
Admissions policies, 81
Admissions Testing Program National Report, 20
Adults
      basic education programs, 25, 26
      learners, 61
Affirmative action, 45–46, 48
African-American students
      academic support services, 37
      demography, 80
Afro-American Literature (course), 38
Alabama: college placement standards, 10
American Association of Community and Junior Colleges, 34
American Indians (see Native Americans)
Analytical and Critical Reading (course), 39
Analytical Reading and Reasoning, 63
Appalachian State University, 78
Arkansas: college placement standards, 10, 11
Assessment: statewide, 74
Attrition: cause, 39

B

Basic skills
      and thinking skills, 68
      instruction, 64
      services, 30
      test, 39
Basic Skills Exam, 80
Black Experience in America (course), 39
Black students (see African-American students)
Bloom's taxonomy, 63
Bridge Program model, 75
"Buddy" systems, 27
Burnout, 44
Business collaboration, 75

C

California: public policy, 73
Campus assistance centers, 23–24

Tutoring
        and remedial programs, 23, 25
        evaluation of, 56
        tutor role, 41
Two-year colleges (see Community colleges)

U
Underprepared college students
        early, 2
        support service need, 5
Underachievers, 4
University of Minnesota, 37–38
University of Missouri, 25
University of Southern California, 27
University of Wisconsin, 1
University role, 74
University System of Georgia, 9, 15, 52, 80

V
Vassar College, 1, 2
Virginia
        admission standards, 6
        college placement standards, 10
Visiting scholars program, 78

W
West Virginia: college placement standards, 10
"Whole student" approach, 37
World War II, 2

Y
Yale University, 2

Since 1983, the Association for the Study of Higher Education (ASHE) and the Educational Resources Information Center (ERIC) Clearinghouse on Higher Education, a sponsored project of the School of Education and Human Development at The George Washington University, have cosponsored the *ASHE-ERIC Higher Education Report* series. The 1989 series is the eighteenth overall and the first to be published by the School of Education and Human Development at the George Washington University.

Each monograph is the definitive analysis of a tough higher education problem, based on thorough research of pertinent literature and insitutional experiences. Topics are identified by a national survey. Noted practitioners and scholars are then commissioned to write the reports, with experts providing critical reviews of each manuscript before publication.

Eight monographs (10 before 1985) in the ASHE-ERIC Higher Education Report series are published each year and are available on a individual or subscription basis. Subscription to eight issues is $80.00 annually; $60 to members of AAHE, AIR, or AERA; and $50 to ASHE members. All foreign subscribers must include an additional $10 per series year for postage.

Prices for single copies, including book rate postage, are $15.00 regular and $11.25 for members of AERA, AIR, AAHE, and ASHE ($10.00 regular and $7.50 for members for 1985 to 1987 reports, $7.50 regular and $6.00 for members for 1983 and 1984 reports, $6.50 regular and $5.00 for members for reports published before 1982). All foreign orders must include $1.00 per book for foreign postage. Fast United Parcel Service or first class postage is available for $1.00 per book in the U.S. and $2.50 per book outside the U.S. (orders above $50.00 may substitue 5% of the total invoice amount for domestic postage). Make checks payable to ASHE-ERIC. For VISA and MasterCard payments, include card number, expiration date, and signature. Orders under $25 must be prepaid. Bulk discounts are avilable on order of 15 or more reports (not applicable to subscription orders). Order from the Publications Department, ASHE-ERIC Higher Education Reports, The George Washington University, One Dupont Circle, Suite 630, Washington, DC 20036-1183, or phone us at (202) 296-2597. Write for a complete catalog of all available reports.

1989 ASHE-ERIC Higher Education Reports

1. Making Sense of Administrative Leadership: The 'L' Word in Higher Education
   Estela M. Bensimon, Anna Neumann, and Robert Birnbaum

2. Affirmative Rhetoric, Negative Action: African-American and Hispanic Faculty at Predominantly White Universities
   Valora Washington and William Harvey

3. Postsecondary Developmental Programs: A Traditional Agenda with New Imperatives
   Louise M. Tomlinson

1988 ASHE-ERIC Higher Education Reports

1. The Invisible Tapestry: Culture in American Colleges and Universities
   George D. Kuh and Elizabeth J. Whitt

2. Critical Thinking: Theory, Research, Practice, and Possibilities
   Joanne Gainen Kurfiss

3. Developing Academic Programs: The Climate for Innovation
   Daniel T. Seymour

4. Peer Teaching: To Teach is To Learn Twice
   Neal A. Whitman

5. Higher Education and State Governments: Renewed Partnership, Cooperation, or Competition?
   Edward R. Hines

6. Entrepreneurship and Higher Education: Lessons for Colleges, Universities, and Industry
   James S. Fairweather

7. Planning for Microcomputers in Higher Education: Strategies for the Next Generation
   Reynolds Ferrante, John Hayman, Mary Susan Carlson, and Harry Phillips

8. The Challenge for Research in Higher Education: Harmonizing Excellence and Utility
   Alan W. Lindsay and Ruth T. Neumann

1987 ASHE-ERIC Higher Education Reports

1. Incentive Early Retirement Programs for Faculty: Innovative Responses to a Changing Environment
   Jay L. Chronister and Thomas R. Kepple, Jr.

2. Working Effectively with Trustees: Building Cooperative Campus Leadership
   Barbara E. Taylor

3. Formal Recognition of Employer-Sponsored Instruction: Conflict and Collegiality in Postsecondary Education
   Nancy S. Nash and Elizabeth M. Hawthorne

4. Learning Styles: Implications for Improving Educational Practices
   Charles S. Claxton and Patricia H. Murrell

5. Higher Education Leadership: Enhancing Skills through Professional Development Programs
   Sharon A. McDade

6. Higher Education and the Public Trust: Improving Stature in Colleges and Universities
   Richard L. Alfred and Julie Weissman

7. College Student Outcomes Assessment: A Talent Development Perspective
   Maryann Jacobi, Alexander Astin, and Frank Ayala, Jr.

8. Opportunity from Strength: Strategic Planning Clarified with Case Examples
   Robert G. Cope

1986 ASHE-ERIC Higher Education Reports

1. Post-tenure Faculty Evaluation: Threat or Opportunity?
   Christine M. Licata

2. Blue Ribbon Commissions and Higher Education: Changing Academe from the Outside
   Janet R. Johnson and Laurence R. Marcus

3. Responsive Professional Education: Balancing Outcomes and Opportunities
   Joan S. Stark, Malcolm A. Lowther, and Bonnie M.K. Hagerty

4. Increasing Students' Learning: A Faculty Guide to Reducing Stress among Students
   Neal A. Whitman, David C. Spendlove, and Claire H. Clark

5. Student Financial Aid and Women: Equity Dilemma?
   Mary Moran

6. The Master's Degree: Tradition, Diversity, Innovation
   Judith S. Glazer

7. The College, the Constitution, and the Consumer Student: Implications for Policy and Practice
   Robert M. Hendrickson and Annette Gibbs

8. Selecting College and University Personnel: The Quest and the Question
   Richard A. Kaplowitz

1985 ASHE-ERIC Higher Education Reports

1. Flexibility in Academic Staffing: Effective Policies and Practices
   Kenneth P. Mortimer, Marque Bagshaw, and Andrew T. Masland

2. Associations in Action: The Washington, D.C. Higher Education Community
   Harland G. Bloland

3. And on the Seventh Day: Faculty Consulting and Supplemental Income
   Carol M. Boyer and Darrell R. Lewis

4. Faculty Research Performance: Lessons from the Sciences and Social Sciences
   John W. Creswell

5. Academic Program Review: Institutional Approaches, Expectations, and Controversies
   Clifton F. Conrad and Richard F. Wilson

6. Students in Urban Settings: Achieving the Baccalaureate Degree
   Richard C. Richardson, Jr. and Louis W. Bender

7. Serving More Than Students: A Critical Need for College Student Personnel Services
   Peter H. Garland

8. Faculty Participation in Decision Making: Necessity or Luxury?
   Carol E. Floyd

1984 ASHE-ERIC Higher Education Reports

1. Adult Learning: State Policies and Institutional Practices
   K. Patricia Cross and Anne-Marie McCartan

2. Student Stress: Effects and Solutions
   Neal A. Whitman, David C. Spendlove, and Claire H. Clark

3. Part-time Faulty: Higher Education at a Crossroads
   Judith M. Gappa

4. Sex Discrimination Law in Higher Education: The Lessons of the Past Decade
   J. Ralph Lindgren, Patti T. Ota, Perry A. Zirkel, and Nan Van Gieson

5. Faculty Freedoms and Institutional Accountability: Interactions and Conflicts
   Steven G. Olswang and Barbara A. Lee

6. The High Technology Connection: Academic/Industrial Cooperation for Economic Growth
   Lynn G. Johnson

7. Employee Educational Programs: Implications for Industry and Higher Education
   Suzanne W. Morse

8. Academic Libraries: The Changing Knowledge Centers of Colleges and Universities
   Barbara B. Moran

9. Futures Research and the Strategic Planning Process: Implications for Higher Education
   James L. Morrison, William L. Renfro, and Wayne I. Boucher

10. Faculty Workload: Research, Theory, and Interpretation
    Harold E. Yuker

1983 ASHE-ERIC Higher Education Reports

1. The Path to Excellence: Quality Assurance in Higher Education
   Laurence R. Marcus, Anita O. Leone, and Edward D. Goldberg

2. Faculty Recruitment, Retention, and Fair Employment: Obligations and Opportunities
   John S. Waggaman

3. Meeting the Challenges: Developing Faculty Careers*
   Michael C.T. Brooks and Katherine L. German

4. Raising Academic Standards: A Guide to Learning Improvement
   Ruth Talbott Keimig

5. Serving Learners at a Distance: A Guide to Program Practices
   Charles E. Feasley

6. Competence, Admissions, and Articulation: Returning to the Basics in Higher Education
   Jean L. Preer

7. Public Service in Higher Education: Practices and Priorities
   Patricia H. Crosson

8. Academic Employment and Retrenchment: Judicial Review and Administrative Action
   Robert M. Hendrickson and Barbara A. Lee

9. Burnout: The New Academic Disease*
   Winifred Albizu Melendez and Rafael M. de Guzmán

10. Academic Workplace: New Demands, Heightened Tensions
    Ann E. Austin and Zelda F. Gamson

*Out-of-print. Available through EDRS. Call 1-800-227-ERIC.

ORDER FORM

Quantity   **Amount**

_____ Please begin my subscription to the 1989 *ASHE-ERIC Higher Education Reports* at $80.00, 33% off the cover price, starting with Report 1, 1989   _____

_____ Please begin my subscription to the 1990 *ASHE-ERIC Higher Education Reports* at $80.00 starting with Report 1, 1990   _____

_____ Outside the U.S., add $10 per series for postage   _____

Individual reports are avilable at the following prices:

1988 and forward, $15   1983 and 1984, $7.50
1985 to 1987, $10   1982 and back, $6.50

Book rate postage within the U.S. is included. Outside U.S., please add $1 per book for postage. Fast U.P.S. shipping is available within the U.S. at $1 per book; outside the U.S., $2.50 per book; orders over $50 may add 5% of the invoice total. All orders under $25 must be prepaid.

PLEASE SEND ME THE FOLLOWING REPORTS:

Quantity	Report No.	Year	Title	Amount

Subtotal:	
Postage(optional):	
Total Due:	

Please check one of the following:
☐ Check enclosed, payable to GWU-ERIC.
☐ Purchase order attached.
☐ Charge my credit card indicated below:
☐ Visa   ☐ MasterCard

Expiration Date _____

Name _____

Title _____

Institution _____

Address _____

City _____ State _____ Zip _____

Phone _____

Signature _____

SEND ALL ORDERS TO:
ASHE-ERIC Higher Education Reports
The George Washington University
One Dupont Circle, Suite 630
Washington, DC 20036-1183
Phone: (202) 296-2597